West Side Pride

West Side Pride

The Cross-Town Rivalry That Created
Four Consecutive Championship Seasons

Warren Western Reserve High School's Journey
To Become Ohio's First Football Playoff Champions

James Carey

Independently Published in
the United States of America

Emerald Bay, LLC
Scottsdale, Arizona

ISBN: 979-8-9864519-0-9 (Hardcover)
Library of Congress Number: 2022910958

For Chris

See them coming down the field,

Gold and White forever!

We will never lose a game,

Because we always fight together!

Kick that ball and catch that pass,

Raiders to Victory!

Fight! Fight! Win Tonight!

We're behind you all the way!

Warren Western Reserve High School Fight Song

CONTENTS

PORTENT

"Poor old Granddad, I laughed at all his words"
From *Ooh La La* by the Faces

The year 2022 marks the fiftieth anniversary of Ohio's very first football playoff championship. That championship was won by Warren Western Reserve High School in 1972, in just the seventh year of its mere 24-year existence. They didn't win simply because they were the most talented team in the state or because they had some of the best coaches in the state, both of which they did. The championship was an archetypical team effort, made possible by the unique rivalry between WWR and Warren's other public high school, Warren G. Harding High. Prior to this, in their first four meetings, the upstart WWR had won the first three games, fomenting a profound but ultimately short-lived competitiveness between the Raiders and the long-established Harding Panthers that led both of them to championships.

Reviewing newspaper accounts of the time will summarily explain which teams were in the first playoffs and who won. Yet unfortunately, the real story has been lost to history. Who won it, the people involved, and how a school won in the fall of only its seventh year is the real story. The story of the first state football playoff champions is that of a decidedly human endeavor; a great team effort by young men playing what has been called the ultimate team sport. It's a story of overcoming adversity, but more than anything else, it is a story of a fabled and now vanquished cross-town rivalry between two high schools in the same small city that set the possibility in motion.

It's likely that nearly every adult has a story or two to tell about their high school days, but few of them have had those days tinged with history. Even fewer of those few have had to watch the history and memory of something notable being gradually, if not systematically, erased as if it never happened. Ask anyone who the Pottsville Maroons were and you will get blank stares. Ask someone from Pottsville Pennsylvania who the Maroons were and they will proudly tell you that they were the 1925 champions of the fledgling National Football League[1]. If you look up the Pottsville Maroons via the internet, you will find a large number of sites that either confirm or dispute Pottsville's claims. But if you search for Warren Western Reserve High School, you will find almost nothing. Much of what you will find will be references to Warren's other legacy high school. Despite what passes for facts and real information on the internet in early 2022, Warren Western Reserve did exist, and its place in Ohio's sports history is irrefutable.

* * * * *

The Ohio High School Athletic Association first used a playoff system to determine Ohio's high school football champion in the fall of 1972, in each of three classes, based on enrollment. A playoff format had been long overdue. From 1895 through 1946, Ohio's champion was not elected or chosen, but simply declared by popular acclaim; effectively by that team's nearest newspaper. On rare occasions, that high school might offer a challenge to any takers, which may or may not have resulted in a late season matchup to decide the matter. For the most part however, the process was merely just a matter of an entity such as the *Plain Dealer* or the *Akron Beacon Journal* anointing a team as the state champion. It is admittedly difficult, however, to argue the run of championships during this period by Paul Brown's Massillon Tigers from 1935 to 1940, whose teams finished 58-1-1 in those six seasons, particularly when Brown's later successes at the college and pro levels is considered.

However, in 1947 this somewhat arbitrary process was replaced. From 1947 through 1971, the state football champion was decided by a poll of Ohio's Associated Press writers (and later paired with the United Press International poll of coaches). Even

---

[1] In 1925, the National Football League featured teams in Akron OH, Hammond IN, Duluth MN, and several other small cities, including Pottsville PA.

before the advent of the high school playoff system, these poll champions were often referred to as having won the "mythical title." A playoff system would solve at least part of the uncertainty surrounding the presumed champion. Ironically, and of more relevance to the story, Warren G. Harding High School – for the first and only time in their history - in 1971 won the very last AP/UPI title bestowed before the beginning of the playoff championship system.

The foundational story of the rivalry between Warren, Ohio's two public high schools' football teams is in many ways unique. Although high school football had been played in Warren since 1892, at the start of the school year in the fall of 1972, Warren Western Reserve, the second of Warren's two public high schools, was just beginning its seventh year of existence. A football rivalry had been fueled from the beginning by the old guard Warren G. Harding High's inability to beat the newcomer school in any of the first three meetings between 1968 and 1970. The teams did not play each other in WWR's first two years. Western Reserve's first loss to Harding in its sixth year and fourth meeting was a bitter wake-up call, particularly as Harding continued that season undefeated and was declared 1971's AP/UPI champion. It was not as if, up to that point, either school had a legacy to defend or to build upon, other than Harding High's place as the high school that had graduated a great many generations of Warren's citizens. The children and grandchildren of many of those graduates were now trying to build a life and a new legacy on the west side of the city.

Until 1971, Harding had not ever, in nearly eighty years of playing high school football, gone undefeated and untied in a season. The school first known as Warren High School was established in 1855, and for reasons not entirely apparent and despite his scandalous administration, was eventually named after our 29th President. It is believed the naming of the school occurred with the construction of a newer, more substantive high school building which opened in 1926. While Harding, the President, was from Ohio, he had no known direct connection to Warren, the city. For a time, the school's teams were even called the Presidents,

3

until Harding adopted the nickname Black Panthers (usually shortened to Panthers) in 1948, and by which they were known until the two Warren schools re-integrated due to falling enrollment in 1990. As Warren High School, the legacy high school that would eventually bear the former President's name first played football in 1892 and eventually in 1963, both helped organize and became a member of the state's elite All-American Football Conference. Yet, until 1971, Harding had largely basked in the glow of its storied conference rivals. The All-American Conference featured among others, Canton McKinley High and Massillon High, the latter where Paul Brown used to dominate Ohio high school football before moving on to success at Ohio State and then to Cleveland's second NFL team[2], which was named for him. However from 1892 until 1971, Harding had never even won outright any conference in which they had played.

Western Reserve opened in the fall of 1966 as a brand new school. Although playing in the upstart North East Ohio Conference and much to Harding's dismay, Western Reserve found almost immediate success in football. Member schools of the NEOC were typically from Akron and Cleveland or their suburbs; all centers of heavy industry. This intensifying rivalry, along with a confluence of physical talent, coaching, teamwork, and the support of the community would result in one or the other of Warren's teams winning a football championship for the next four years in a row, from 1971-1974. The rivalry between the schools set the championship run in motion, as each school became obsessed with beating the other. Notable, because for three of those four years, the winner of Warren's rivalry game ultimately also ended the regular season undefeated and in all four subsequently as the state's champion, in one form or another. The rivalry game was scheduled each year in the fifth week of the season for more than a decade, which was likely out of deference to Harding's legacy obligations as a member of the premier All-American Conference. Later however, the importance to both

---

[2] The Rams were originally established in Cleveland, before they moved to Los Angeles, Anaheim, St. Louis, and back to Los Angeles.

teams had become more than self-evident, and the rival game was moved to the final game of the regular season. Nearly everyone from either school when they weren't using more colorful language referred to the other as their "cross-town rival." In the early 70s, the momentum of a win in week five did a lot to energize the team's confidence and resolve, and to allow the possibilities ahead to come into view. However, winning the rivalry game, regardless of either team's final record, would be considered a successful season. The uniqueness and intensity of the rivalry did not escape the notice of the Cleveland *Plain Dealer*, Ohio's largest city's newspaper. The *Plain Dealer* usually featured the upcoming game a few days before with a full-page spread, typically including both schools' team photos and interviews with the coaches.

Not that we as Americans are all that hung up on details in most cases. Of late, people seem considerably more content with being told how they should feel about things rather than knowing about them, so as to be able to make up their own minds. But when nearly all of the details are wiped clean, people have no reason to care one way or the other. Unfortunately, it seems that much of the story of the first state champs has slowly but progressively been relegated to a literal footnote in local history - if at all - and more unfortunately, so has the legacy of the men who made this happen. The story is being lost through time and by the passing of several of the men who won that very first Ohio High School Athletic Association trophy. Lost through the token expressions of what passes for communication these days. Lost through obliteration of the physical structures that were central and vital to winning the championship. Today in fact, most online references - what few exist - to the men on WWR's first playoff championship team indicate they had gone to and graduated from Warren G. Harding. This is tangible proof that people are willingly or obligingly ignoring their past. These references are not only incorrect, they are insulting to those who lived and helped create and sustain the rivalry.

How did this happen? In 1990, when the re-integration of the two schools occurred, it was decided that WWR would close and

Harding would once again become Warren's sole public high school. The physical structure that was Warren G. Harding High School was 64 years old at the time. Thus, Warren Western Reserve High School, after a mere 24 years as Warren's second high school, was about to become extinct: repurposed in 1990 and then razed completely in 2010 – after a brand new Harding High had been built in 2008. All of WWR's athletic facilities and anything that might even hint at its existence, let alone its significance, are gone. Because of this, there is no reference point; there is no reason to care and most importantly, no reason to learn from it. You can't go to the school, or to where the school was to see any hint that anything was even there, or that anything unique ever happened there. Upon re-integration of the two schools, the solitary concessions to the existence of anything other than Harding High as Warren's only high school were that WWR's gold and white colors and its team name 'Raiders' would replace the Harding Panthers' red and white. This is something that had already happened at least twice in Harding's history and something of which very few are likely even aware. Conveniently if not coincidentally, even though renaming the team Raiders, the depiction was changed: WGH's Raider is different from WWR's Raider. Everything else was gone and quickly overlooked, which undoubtedly was the entire idea, or it would not have happened as it did. But: The person or persons who decided to do these things grossly and entirely squandered the significance of both of the schools by doing what they were doing; in essence, sending both the city's 'step-school' and the rivalry into oblivion.

Most important to the story – literally vital– is that along with the people and the physical facilities, the rivalry is gone. It is gone and quickly fading from memory and therefore from significance. Without the cross-town rivalry between these two schools, the four year run of championships almost certainly would not have happened. One needs only to review the record of mediocrity that Warren's single high school teams had for nearly 80 years to strongly deduce such. It is entirely possible that *none* of the championships would have happened. And correspondingly, because the rivalry did exist, without appreciating the rivalry, one cannot understand how and why the run of championships happened at all. Should this happen - and unfortunately it has - its significance diminishes with it, and that should not be permitted let alone encouraged by obliterating the physical artifacts and memory of a formidable rival. The story of the rivalry is an incredibly valuable object lesson, the embodiment of the oft-paraphrased admonition to the world in its simplest terms: We learn from history that we don't learn from history. To understand the incredible success these teams had, the rivalry needs to be understood, *especially* by the people of Warren and Northeast Ohio. Any attempts to destroy the memory and legacy of WWR are a colossal mistake. It isn't only the school and any achievements its students and staff might have made that should be remembered and celebrated. It is the *irreplaceable* cross-town rivalry.

As west siders, maybe we should have seen it coming. Perhaps a portent of what was to occur was right there in plain sight for everyone to see, right from the beginning. One of those mystical coincidences seething in ironic hindsight is that in the mere twenty four academic years that WWR existed as Warren's second public high school, it operated from September to May each of those years for a total very close to exactly two hundred months. The school's address was 200 Loveless Avenue.

The story herein however, is that of Ohio's first state football champs. To be more precise, it is the story of the first Class AAA *(Translation: large enrollment school)* Ohio High School playoff champions. And just for edification; along the way to that championship, WWR defeated the team that would be the Class AA champs earlier that season somewhat decisively by a score of 36-20. A rival in the same North East Ohio Conference, this speaks to the quality of play in that conference at that time. One team would be standing on top when the final gun sounded. One team would be first. That team was the 1972 Warren Western Reserve Raiders.

Fifty years on, it is time to preserve the memory of a significant moment in Ohio sports history. To understand the story of the

Ohio's first state champs, it is necessary to put it into its proper time and place. Warren's combined four championship years were the same four that I was a student at Western Reserve, and as a sophomore and junior, a member of the football team. As a result, I witnessed firsthand the highs and the lows of the rivalry, got a concussion or two along the way, broke a chip off a bone in my hand, and all the while learned an incredible amount about teamwork, leadership, and the game of football.

If you're looking for salacious stories or harsh criticisms within these pages, you will be disappointed. However, I do comment on a thing or two and any criticisms I provide here and there are both direct and truthful. The players and even the coaches were more socially disciplined then and pretty much only did what is referred to as 'Johnny Carson swearing': a lot of hells and damns, but that was about it, aside from when they were in outright fights or similar situations. This alone might illustrate how different things were 50 years ago and signals that we as a nation have certainly gone a long way in at least one direction that might not necessarily be viewed as progress.

Warren was pretty much where the Midwest started in the early 1970s (albeit the industrial Midwest) and where a lot of people not more than a few minutes away still owned and operated farms. But by this time, Warren and surrounding environs had primarily become a center of industrial production. My friend John DiGiacobbe used to tag onto Cleveland's prideful slogan as "The Best Location in the Nation" by noting that the industrial production in the area would put Northeast Ohio among the (then) Soviet Union's number one targets, should they ever decide to nuke the U.S. Maybe there's an aphorism about lemons and lemonade in there somewhere? Steel, aluminum, autos and auto parts, and numerous other supporting industries provided an employment base to pursue the American dream, in whatever form one might see that. But also by this time, the writing was on the wall and this economic base was threatened by labor unrest, foreign competition, and outdated production technologies, or at least that's where people would place the blame. Oversimplification seems to have become another aspect of the

American Way, however. The result in any case, is that the challenges the people of the area would face in the coming years would be significant and would persist for decades. The persistent and determined character of Warren's population also marked its football teams.

More than anything, this story is about the people who succeeded against the odds. So, amongst the necessary details are my recollections of both the players and coaches peppering the discussions of the road to Ohio's first playoff football championship. The short version of how it all came together is that it was convergence of fortune: one small city, talented football players, in the right place, at the right time, with the right coaches, in fierce competition with a proximate rival, at the moment in time when the system in which the sport they played underwent a tectonic change. This wave of change would be thanks to a cash register repairman from one of the numerous bedroom communities east of Cleveland.

1

BACKSTORY

Fifty years after Ohio's first football playoff championship, the world has become a very different place, and thus it is necessary to begin with some context. The 1970 Census indicated that the population of Warren was about 63,000, which is considerably more than the 2020 Census indicates at 39,200. Even then, this made Warren - at least by comparison with nearby Youngstown, Akron, or Cleveland - a small city. Warren had only one radio station, and the closest network television stations were in Youngstown, 15 miles or so to the southeast. To tune to the correct station channel, you physically turned the UHF dial on your TV set. The TV remote of the day was usually the youngest member of the family, who was told to go change the channel, which is as analog as it gets. What's a UHF dial? An actual round and numbered knob, this was one of two round dials you turned on your TV set to select a channel number corresponding to the station number, the other being the VHF dial. It was mechanical, not electronic, and so it made a *clunk, clunk* sound as you turned each number on the dial. This was not unlike the dial on virtually all telephones at the time which had to be rotated in a correct seven-number sequence to reach your intended local party.

Every telephone was still firmly attached to a wall, or to a cord that was attached to a wall and you paid extra for a private line. More notably, during phone conversations people regularly asked, "How are you?" This has clearly gone the way of the dinosaur and replaced by, "Where are you?" The other aspect of 1970s phones was that when the phone rang, you never knew who was calling. "Caller ID" would not become mainstream for more than another decade. In fact, I distinctly remember talking to a telephone repairman who had just climbed down from a pole in 1982. For some reason I observed, "I bet you can't wait until all these phone lines are gone." His response word-for-word was, "Oh, that'll never happen."

Black-and-white photos and television sets were still prevalent. There was no ESPN, or Google, or Amazon. No cell phones, personal computers, or just about any convenience you have today and probably can't imagine living without. *The Simpsons* would not come to television screens for another 20 years; but amazingly are still making new episodes after 30 years on the air. Here's the part that really puts things in perspective, however: Neil Armstrong gets virtually all the credit, but there were actually six Apollo missions that landed a total of twelve men on the moon and the last four of those moon landings occurred in 1971 and 1972. If Buzz Aldrin hadn't been on *Dancing with the Stars* in 2010, most people still probably wouldn't know who he was when he walked down the street. *(Well, that and the time he punched a guy on the street in front of television cameras.)* So, the fiftieth anniversary of Ohio's first state football championship coincides within a month of the fiftieth anniversary of the last time an American - or anyone else - walked on the moon. Or rather, as Apollo 16's Commander John Young insisted, "I didn't *walk* on the moon, I *worked* on the moon!"[3]

Elvis was still very much alive and selling out venues regularly. The "King of Rock'n'Roll", was an icon of popular culture at the time, but unfortunately Elvis's legacy has long been relegated to summary judgments about less meaningful aspects of his life, such as how he (eventually) died, whether or not he actually died, his weight, his eating habits, etc. Some say the 70s were lost years for rock music, perhaps because the disco craze spoiled the fun for purists in the latter part of the decade. But none of that was Elvis's fault, even though he had already started losing much of his luster once the British invasion of the '60s had begun. Author Mike Edison, a rock music historian says more succinctly in his book *Sympathy for the Drummer*, "Every rock'n'roll band in the country owed Elvis a great debt. ... It's a tragedy that American youth in

[3] Kelly, Scott, (2017). *Endurance.* NY: Mach 25/Penguin Random House , pg. 212.

1972 spent more money on the Doobie Brothers than on Elvis, but that was the state of rock'n'roll culture."[4]

Star Trek had already come, underwhelmed, and gone. Funny thing though, the show's three seasons were syndicated and effectively ubiquitous on the few TV channels you likely received, so you could watch them practically any day of the week. A following developed that was considerably more whelmed this time around. It took until the start of the next decade, but the franchise would recover from its initial TV cancelation quite nicely.

'Apple' was either the first page of a children's book on the alphabet, or the name of the company the Beatles had formed to try to actually start earning some money for themselves, rather than primarily making other people rich. It had nothing to do with the phone you used or the music you listened to, and a computer at the time was something that filled part of a large room, cost tens of thousands of dollars, and used huge reels of magnetic tape and piles of punch cards to do what we would now consider some of the most mundane tasks. The business that would start in a garage with the same name and which would become the first trillion dollar company (*That's trillion with a "Tr"*) did not yet exist.

Art Fleming was still the original host of Jeopardy, which featured a manually operated board and clues worth something like a whopping $25. If you are reading this and remember Art Fleming from anything other than Weird Al Yankovic's *Jeopardy* parody, I regret to inform you that you are officially old. John Wayne was still making westerns. Sean Connery had just returned as James Bond, but Roger Moore was shortly to appear, upon which the eternal debate would begin: Who's the best Bond? Very early in 1971, the Super Bowl was only up to V, and is most notable as very possibly being the only Super Bowl that will ever have the game's Most Valuable Player come from the losing team: Dallas Cowboys linebacker Chuck Howley. If it didn't happen twenty years later in 1991, when Buffalo Bills running back Thurman Thomas almost single-handedly made an actual football

---

[4] Edison, Mike. (2019). *Sympathy for the Drummer: Why Charlie Watts Matters.* Lanham MD: Backbeat Books, pp.232-233.

game out of Super Bowl XXV despite the loss, it never will. Apparently, whoever voted for such things at the time was quite anxious to get home, and decided well before the game was over that the Cowboys would defeat the Colts. They did not. They did return in January of 1972 to finish the job, however.

The point of the contextual trip down memory lane is that in the early 1970s the world in general and Warren Ohio in particular were decidedly analog compared to our day to day existence in the 21st Century. Warren was largely a proud blue collar town, but not without its claims to fame. In addition to Paul Warfield, Randy Gradishar of nearby Champion, Bill Kollar, several of the Browner clan (Ross, Jim, Joey, Keith) and later Korey Stringer and Mario Manningham - who all played in the NFL - were born there. Catherine Bach (Daisy Duke) and Austin Pendleton were born there. Yes, you might not recognize the name, but you know who he is. Pendleton, a Harding grad, was the evil Charles Durning's sidekick in *The Muppet Movie*, and also played the stuttering lawyer who is fired by Ralph Macchio's friend in favor of Joe Pesci in *My Cousin Vinnie*. Much more famous on Broadway, you've seen him in movies and television for years. Foo fans know that Dave Grohl was also born there. Thus, incredible as it may seem, grunge roots extend all the way to Northeast Ohio. His family moved away as a small child, but his life began in Warren. He is very likely the only person from Warren in the Rock & Roll Hall of Fame ... and he's been inducted twice.

Ron Parise, astronaut and veteran of two NASA shuttle missions, was from Warren. And even though he wasn't born there, Neil Armstrong (perhaps the one astronaut you do recognize) made a giant leap to immortality when, as a six year old, he took his very first airplane ride in Warren. A commemorative site now marks the spot on Parkman Road where an airfield once existed, one that most people even in 1969 when Armstrong was taking a much more historic flight, had long forgotten. A bar housed in a weathered red Quonset hut was a curious relic of the field and of that era at the time, and of which most people did not bother to notice on their way to and from the neighboring K-Mart. Neil Armstrong's father worked as an auditor for the state and the family had lived in Warren for a time. The exact day in July of 1936 is debated, but accounts agree that the first man to step on the moon once lived in Warren, and had his very first aviation experience there when his father bought them tickets for a ride in a Ford Tri-Motor.

Most of Northeast Ohio was industrial, and people largely adhered to a strong work ethic, something that undoubtedly gave all of these people some of their drive to succeed. Warren is located in what was, in early the 1970s, a swath of industrial production that extended from Pittsburgh to Detroit and then pretty much continued the rest of the way to Chicago. Large steel and tire manufacturing complexes, auto manufacturers, and supporting industries were huge contributors to the employment base of the region. It was not unusual to awaken any given morning on Warren's south side and find a coating of very black coarse dust on everything in sight, including any car that had not been garaged. This was a particularly vexing sight in the winter if it had first snowed, whereupon this odd black layer would have been deposited on top of the fresh white snow. But at least the latter circumstance was less harmful for your car's paint, and made it much easier to clean off. The coating was courtesy of the coke processing operations, which were both adjacent to and necessary for one of the major steel producers south of the city which manufactured steel from raw iron ore. In this case, coke has nothing to do with Coca-Cola. Coke is the term for processed coal used in making steel from iron ore. Coincidentally however, there also was a fairly small Coca-Cola bottling facility on Parkman Road, which was soon destined to cease operations around this same time. Hence, few people even remember it was there, but I knew a guy who worked there loading trucks after school. I wonder if the people working today at Warren Design & Build are aware of the building's history. Unfortunately, the decline and closure of much of the employment base was also the case for many of the larger employers of the city and the region. Industrial production had crested around this time. Labor unrest, foreign competition, and cost increases would also soon contribute to many of these backbone industries reducing or curtailing operations altogether, and many of the names are nearly lost to history.

Take drinking fountains, which had been effectively ubiquitous. Many, especially those in public buildings, were made in Warren. It was amusing to be somewhere like San Francisco, or Ft Lauderdale, or Tempe Arizona and right where the fountain drained was a chrome ring that read "Halsey Taylor Warren Ohio." Its products may have been ubiquitous at one time, but it too would eventually leave Warren. The company was purchased and effectively absorbed by Elkay, which still operates in Illinois. You can still buy Halsey Taylor fountains, but they no longer are made in, nor say "Warren Ohio." Slowly therefore, job opportunities and expectations for graduates in 1970 and 1971 were very different from those available just a couple years later in 1974 and 1975. To the south, Youngstown was soon to be particularly hard hit with massive closures and the complete razing of large steel producing complexes.

General Motors had a large presence in the area with an assembly plant in nearby Lordstown, and with Packard Electric (which much later became Delphi). The latter was a large manufacturing facility that made electrical devices such as wiring harnesses and fiber optic cables for many of GM's and some other auto manufacturer's assembly plants. The Packard family, for whom the plant was named, began building cars in Warren before the turn of the 20th century. Yes, the first Packard autos were made in Warren. Although Packard Motor Company's operations moved to Detroit shortly afterward in 1903, the Packard family legacy in Warren remains in the form of a large city park for which the family had donated the land, and upon which sits the W.D. Packard Music Hall. Every summer from 1958 until 1977, John Kenley began his Kenley Players summer stock theatre tours at Packard Music Hall. If you watched *Hollywood Squares* on television at the time, at the end of the Friday show, Peter Marshall would occasionally ask, for example, Rose Marie or Paul Lynde what they were doing or where they would be that weekend, and sometimes Warren, Ohio would get a national namedrop. From 1958 to 1977, many well-known and some genuinely famous performers spent part of their summers in Warren. Packard Park, which enveloped the music hall, also contoured along the Mahoning River and offered facilities for tennis, baseball, and swimming. Along with those were two duck ponds, handy in winter for ice skating. The Packard family legacy looms large in Warren to this day, and their generosity has benefitted generation after generation of the city's residents, most of whom likely do not know how or why so many things were named Packard.

Timken was a world renowned name in nearby Canton, and its sister city Akron was the home of Firestone, and Goodyear, and General tire. There was little doubt about what the industrial complexes along the freeway in and around Akron were producing; the smell of rubber permeated the air. Cleveland is the nearest large city, in fact the largest in Ohio. A weekend diversion for many was staying up late to watch the *Hoolihan and Big Chuck Show* on one of Cleveland's VHF channels. It was one of the many local programs across the country showing a B- or C-movie that was enhanced because the skits and activities they did during breaks in the movie were often better than the movies they were showing. Bob Wells (Hoolihan) was the station's weather man and sometime actor and "Big" Chuck Schodowski was a producer at the station. They had taken up the mantle from the wildly popular Ghoulardi, who had previously been seen multiple days a week throughout the 60s. Ghoulardi had a fake van dyke mustache and usually wore a goofy hat of some kind that added to the silliness of the whole thing. Ernie Anderson (Ghouldari) left with his friend and associate Tom Conway to work in Los Angeles, and thus the mantle was passed to Hoolihan and Big Chuck to become a weekend staple. Conway changed his name to Tim and both of them eventually ended up on *The Carol Burnett Show*; Tim as a featured player and Ernie as the voice-over announcer.

Cleveland, a major city in all respects, had about that time become a national joke which had nothing to do with their TV programming, or the city being home to large-scale auto and steel manufacturing, or the scientific development being done there at NASA's Lewis (now Glenn) Research Center. Of course, it didn't help that none of the city's professional sports teams were doing particularly well at the time. The Indians were habitually bad and the Browns, although fairly consistent, had the 1964 NFL championship fading quickly in fans' memories. Owner Art Modell was regularly being trashed for his indiscretions of firing head coach and Ohio legend Paul Brown and shortly thereafter trading away Paul Warfield (a Warren native, Ohio State star, and eventual NFL Hall-of-Famer) for a quarterback who was never able to return the team to glory. *OH! If Browns fans only knew what fate the future held!*[5] The Kardiac Kids were still years away and Elway-the-Destroyer wasn't even yet in high school. But the real reason Cleveland was a national joke was that chemical wastes from one or more of the many industrial facilities had been dumped directly into the Cuyahoga River, and in 1969 had, quite literally, caught fire. Cleveland was known around the country and around the world as the city where the river burned. An unbelievable and unconscionable footnote to the story is that it had actually happened more than a dozen times, primarily before the newly burgeoning television news industry, and stand-up comedians everywhere, brought the absurdity of it to everyone's attention.

Adrift in these blue-collar environs were the two most burning questions for current and recent high school students in the early 70s: "When will the Vietnam War be over?" and "When are the Beatles going to get back together?" (Spoiler: They never did.) They had disbanded in 1970. Perhaps you've heard of them? Day in and day out, the networks provided a complete absence of

---

[5] Modell somewhat abruptly moved the team to Baltimore in 1996 to become the Ravens, leaving Cleveland without the NFL team that had been a signature of the city for fifty years. Arguably, he had legitimate reasons for moving, but perhaps not for the way in which he did it. As part of the league agreement to permit the team to move, all Browns' records, history, and intellectual property were placed in a trust in expectation of adoption by another team at a later time. Officially, the Browns were suspended for three years, and then resurrected through expansion.

good news about the war in Southeast Asia and its seemingly obligatory daily body counts, as if abstractly, body counts were scores illustrating that the war was merely some 'game' that we were 'winning'. Many years later we were told the truth; that these body counts were exaggerated – sometimes outrageously – at least as it pertained to the enemy. But at the time, everyone dutifully listened to Walter Cronkite on CBS or to Chet Huntley on NBC and believed what they were told. ABC was exceptional with sports, regularly broadcasting the Olympics every four years, but they were seldom the network you watched for news (or any programming other than sports at the time for that matter). Three networks with a half hour broadcast, all at exactly the same time each evening, and a daily afternoon newspaper from which you found out what had happened yesterday. That was it. No cable networks, no social media, no 24 hour news cycle. Alternatively, if you were more obsessed with the latter question of the day, you probably subscribed to CREEM magazine, self-described as "America's Only Rock-n-Roll Magazine," and published in nearby Detroit, or perhaps to Rolling Stone which had not yet gained its cult status. Like so many other cultural touchstones of the region, CREEM also ultimately folded in 1989, probably because Rolling Stone did manage to gain its cult status to become what Beach Boy Brain Wilson refers to as "rock's arbiter of hip."[6]

As you might expect, there were McDonald's and Dairy Queen restaurants on both sides of town. But food-wise, Warren's claim to fame was the Hot Dog Shoppe, an institution since 1946. Located less than a mile west of the river on the city's primary east-west thoroughfare, the Hot Dog Shoppe was a great place for an inexpensive meal and has for decades been an employer that hires many students from Warren and the surrounding area. With hot dogs grilled on a flattop, their proprietary chili sauce still beats any in the country, although I can't say the same for their French Fries. There must be a story behind the fact that if you order your hot dog "with everything," it comes with chili sauce and onions. If you really wanted "everything" – sauce, onions, mustard,

---

[6] Wilson, B. & Gold, T. (1991). *Wouldn't It Be Nice*. NY: HarperCollins Publishers.

sauerkraut, whatever else – you have to be specific. For Warren and nearby parts of Northeast Ohio, Hot Dog Shoppe's fare was a basic food group. Yes, you can get a hamburger at the Hot Dog Shoppe ... but why would you?

The Hot Dog Shoppe with its unmistakable signage.

Nearby Youngstown was larger and even more dependent upon the steel industry. Many of Warren's high school opponents were from Youngstown and surrounding area. Schools such as Ursuline, Boardman, Chaney, and Austintown Fitch had been on the football schedule of either Harding or Reserve for years. Youngstown also had two gems that drew people from all over the area: Mill Creek Park and Idora Park. Mill Creek Park was a fairly large pastoral area within the city that ran along, of course, Mill Creek. Picnicking and hiking were both draws, but the park also had tennis courts, soccer fields, etc., and was simply a place just to get away and enjoy nature. Idora Park was an amusement park adjacent to Mill Creek Park. It boasted a classic wooden roller coaster called the Wild Cat, which ranked high nationally with enthusiasts. Idora Park Ballroom, which was built in the early part of the 20th Century, became a required stop of big bands and then pop groups for decades. It was old enough to once host the Tommy Dorsey Band which featured a completely unknown singer named Frank Sinatra. Throughout the twentieth century, the Ballroom had seen it all come and go. By the 1970s, the Ballroom was hosting pop groups such as the Monkees, television's answer to the Fab Four, and even lesser and more forgettable groups as state-of-the-art arenas were being built all over the country which provided more enticing options for both fans and performers. A fire in 1984 ended the park's run and its convenient fun for thousands of nearby residents.

Youngstown also became the bellwether of the decline of steel manufacturing in the U.S. Foreign automakers and foreign steel were making steady progress in American markets, and steel manufacturers were beginning to feel the pinch. Even appliance makers were buying cheaper (and subsidized) steel from foreign manufacturers. Work shifts in the massive complexes in and around Youngstown were already starting to be reduced. Specialty steel manufacturers like Copperweld (*odd name for a steel company*) and Thomas Steel continued to carve out a viable business niche, at least for a while. But the writing was on the wall, and many of the gargantuan complexes – along with their jobs - would soon go idle or be torn down entirely.

Within this backdrop were Warren G. Harding and Warren Western Reserve High Schools. Harding had been the backbone of education in the city for decades. Even if you went to "Reserve" as it was called, or "WWR", it was extremely likely that your parents, grandparents, and older siblings, if you had any, graduated from Harding. Harding was just a little north and east of downtown, fairly centrally located, and had the football stadium that both schools used. The stadium was named for Milton Mollenkopf, a longtime teacher, coach, and principal at Harding. Harding played home games on Friday night, and Reserve played home games on Saturday night. Harding also had a wealth of adjacent space. So large was the available space at the time, the Trumbull County Fair used to be held on the grounds each year, along with its abundance of carnival rides and farm animals of all types, all essentially in the middle of the city. In 1973, the city paved over multiple acres of land to the east of Mollenkopf Stadium to build a massive driver education facility that was also to be used by both schools. Underused is a better description however. It was more suited to someone who had never been in a car, with lots of cones delineating parking spaces and gently curving streets, with a ridiculously low speed limit, for which you were yelled at via radio if it even appeared you were violating. Primarily it was useful as a safe place to practice parallel parking, which was every 16-year-old's dreaded portion of the driver's license test, but classmate Paul Tarleton and I more than once did manage some fun on the area that was designated a skid pad. The entire space was later mercifully reimagined, and now houses Harding's baseball field.

Owing to an increase in student population thanks to the baby boom, a new high school opened in Fall of 1966 on the west side of the city that was given the name Warren Western Reserve. The new school's name was derived from Warren's former status as capital of the Connecticut Western Reserve. If you were to extend lines of latitude westward from the north and south boundaries of Connecticut, as it existed in the late 1700's, they would eventually encompass most of what is now northeast Ohio, as it pertains to land area south of Lake Erie. Connecticut made land claims for the region west of Pennsylvania's border in this manner. They called it the Western Reserve, and sold parcels of valuable land to those adventurous enough to settle in the area. Before Ohio became a state in 1803, Warren was the capital of the Western Reserve and the seat of Trumbull County, which it remains today. This reserve of lands, a couple hundred or so years later, included what eventually became the cities of not just Warren, but also Cleveland and Youngstown as well.

Warren was settled on the banks of the Mahoning River. The Mahoning wound its way approximating north and south; passing right next to the Public Square where the Courthouse was eventually built in the center of the city, and thus many years later, the river became the de facto divider that determined which high school you would attend. If you lived east of the river, you went to Harding; west of the river, you would go to WWR. The city had three junior high schools for grades 7 and 8. East and West Junior High students went to their respective geographic high school, but Turner Junior High was newer and more centrally located, so some people with whom you may have gone to school and formed friendships might eventually and abruptly become your sworn enemy once you started high school. It depended upon where you actually lived.

Warren's Courthouse Square on a fall day ... perfect for football.

WWR was, for the mid-1960s, a modern high school, built on available land next to an existing elementary school. It did not have the massive spaces surrounding it, but the space for parking, and practice fields was, at least at first, adequate for the football team. In the spring, the track team practiced indoors if it was too cold, and on the asphalt-paved parking lot when it was warm enough, and most of the cars had gone. Lines for running lanes and circles designating shot put and discus throwing were painted in among the lined parking spaces. Although we sometimes had to wait for the cars to clear out to use the parking lot, I vividly remember a teammate practicing the discus as it went to *the* only place in a couple of acres that it should not have. It landed squarely and loudly, dead center onto the windshield of the absolutely one and only car still in the parking lot. What's more, the driver and his three passengers had just slammed all four doors shut to leave, and an instant later, the windshield was obliterated. At once both scared and livid, all four of them flew out the four doors and every one of them could have taught ex-Navy man Johnny Carson a few new words, even though all of us could not keep from laughing. I am fairly certain that it was genuinely an accident because, let's call him "Russ", seemed upset with himself, though not nearly as upset as the driver and his friends were with him. (Hmm, but now that I think about it ... seems like maybe Russ could have just waited like *one* more minute to throw the thing? I mean, he had to have seen those guys walking to their car....?) Coach Earl strolled somewhat nonchalantly but directly toward the irate driver, and ultimately had to get in his face to calm him down, explaining the school's insurance would pay for his windshield. He then told the guy to just get in his car and leave.

Fairly new, the school was complete and modern in most aspects. It had large, floating Brady Bunch-esque stairwells of steel and concrete, a library, an auditorium, and the windows opened easily in nearly every classroom. There was an Olympic sized pool, a nice gymnasium/basketball court, a complete shop wing for students to take auto body or mechanics, and even a planetarium. I believe it was the only one anywhere nearby, but the only students who ever used it were from the city's elementary schools on a field trip, or the high school band which used it occasionally for practice. Perhaps the acoustics were better, but I suspect they just used it as a place so as not to bother anyone, since quite literally no one was ever in there. They used the parking lot, or the grassy area just west of the school's rear entrance in the summer and fall to practice their marches. The baseball team had to go off property to play or to practice, using the baseball fields at city parks to practice and play games, which Harding did as well. To host a meet, the track teams also used Mollenkopf stadium, the field of which was encircled with what was probably, once-upon-a-time, an old-style cinder track. For the most part really, it was just hard clay. We were thrilled when we went away to track meets in wealthier school districts, or those lucky enough to modernize, which had the new rubberized tracks, having a soft and level running surface, along with the benefit of being weatherproof.

An unpleasant aspect of the school was that getting there was not fun. Several railroad tracks ran east to west on the north side of the school. From the west, it would be a couple miles from the main road to get to the school, the so called 'back way'. However, the main entrance faced east. It was about the same distance from the main road to the school, but the school had been built, for most of that distance, behind a government housing project called Westlawn. Westlawn was purportedly built to support the World War II effort by housing workers for the arsenal located in nearby Ravenna, and which by the early 70s had seen better days. Like any other crowded basic housing project, it featured row upon row of homes, the majority of which shared walls, and many of which were in desperate need of proper care. It was just unsightly, and then *Bam!* There's a new high school hiding behind it all.

Western Reserve High School was an interconnected structure layered in brick. Behind the main front doors, was a common area with the cafeteria and an auditorium for typically more formal collective activities, but pep rallies were also held there on Friday afternoons, where John Scharf the school's principal gamely put on a small native headdress and stirred up the students' enthusiasm. On the northeast side were school offices and the planetarium, the dome of which could easily be seen while driving toward the building. To the southeast was the three-story classroom block, and behind it to the west were the gymnasium and the Olympic-sized pool. On the north side was the shop wing for students learning auto repair or auto body, and the metal shop, etc. The parking lot was north of that. In front of the building was a large rectangular(-*ish*) concrete common area with a raised flag platform. The platform was a level, flat stage also of concrete that was about two feet off the ground and of significant size. It probably hovered over 20-25% of the whole common area. It would seem that its purpose was to give students a place to sit or congregate from time to time when the weather permitted. The flag pole rose up from the middle of the platform.

South of the building structure were a few acres of grass where the football team practiced. There was one field at the very southwestern corner of school property which had actual goalposts and served mostly as a practice field and intermittently as a game field for non-varsity games (freshmen, sophomore, and junior varsity). The field was usually striped with lime in a standard gridiron layout at least once when twice-a-day practices began, but the general outline of yardage and boundaries had been more or less burned into the sparse grass even then. When the weather was or had been bad, we did not use the game field, unless it was necessary in order to practice placekicking, but we used it a lot when it was firm and dry. The adjacent acreage was large enough for two more football fields which were intermittently limed as well once practice started in summer, and which received the bulk of our practice use. The blocking sleds and cages were located on these fields. It was a large enough space allowing coaches and functions to divide up by position, or by offense and defense, or by starters and scout teams, etc.

Such was life as the school year and the high school football season began in the fall of 1971 - the year the rivalry first paid real dividends.

2

15-8

One thing absolutely necessary to play a game of football is a football. The ball we used was a Spalding J5-V, which may beg the question, "Does it matter?" Actually, it does. You may think a football is a football, but that is not true. The term 'football shaped', refers more correctly to a prolate spheroid. Variations in the degree of prolation (if that's a word) create differences between one brand or model of football to another. Some balls had white stripes on them, some did not. Ours did. When it began in the 1960s, the American Football League used Spalding's J5-V with a slight variation, while the NFL was still using Wilson's "The Duke" at the time. The AFL ball was made specifically for the league and included the league logo branded into the leather. Because the ball was made specifically for play in the new league, and although dimensionally the same as the J5-V, it was technically re-designated the J6-V. It was slightly thinner at its maximum girth (the circumference of the fat part of the ball) and had extra padding underneath the leather than did the NFL ball, largely because the AFL intended all along to highly emphasize the passing game. The ever-so-slightly more svelte shape made it easier to grip, making it both easier to throw and easier to catch than the (ever so slightly) fatter Duke.

We used the J5-V in all of our games, except in the playoff games. All playoff teams were required to use the same Wilson ball, probably a variation of their 1001 model, which was clearly slightly fatter than the J5-V. So eleven weeks into the season, everyone was practicing with brand new and marginally different footballs. Or at least the quarterbacks were, because we only had a few of them. Literally after a few minutes, it did not matter. We adjusted very quickly.[7]

Early in the season, I went looking to buy a J5-V, reasoning that since it was the ball we used, it must be easy to find. It wasn't. Most sporting goods stores said they never heard of it, one of them even told me it didn't exist. Of course, one of them had heard of it, but would gladly sell me the one they had on their shelf, whatever it was, because they said, "they were all the same." Different manufacturers not only have different shaped footballs; there are differences in the materials used to make them. Many, like the J5-V, are genuine leather, while others are made using a synthetic or compound, which gives them a semi-permanent tackiness. They solve that conundrum nowadays at all levels by having virtually all receivers wear some variety of silicone gloves. We also could not and did not use "stick um," the goopy glue that once allowed Hall of Fame Oakland Raider receiver Fred Biletnikoff to catch a pass with his forearm.

It took a while (no one had ever yet heard the word "internet") but I finally found one in, of all places, a department store in downtown Youngstown. McKelvey's was a large five or six floor department store, and even then it seemed like something out of an old black-and-white movie. When you rode the elevator, the operator (*can you believe it – a real elevator operator!*) would announce each stop, such as "Fifth Floor, Sporting Goods." That may have been the first and last time I ever actually experienced it, outside of seeing it in an old movie. McKelvey's, and Strouss', and Carlisle's, which were among the notable stores of the area, and all of them would soon be gone, and neither Wal-Mart nor the internet had anything to do with it.

* * * * *

As the Harding Panthers approached the football season of 1971, their focus shifted from their duly-storied rivals in the All

---

[7] The shape of the football has changed considerably over the game's evolution. Peyton Manning, in an excellent episode of *Peyton's Places*, shows the changes to the NFL ball and the difference of the pre-merger AFL ball, including how much harder/easier it is to catch or throw the different footballs.

American Conference such as Massillon, Niles, and Canton McKinley. Harding had their sights firmly fixed on their cross-town rival, Western Reserve. And it was this cross-town rivalry that led to something that had never been done before in Warren Ohio.

Warren Western Reserve did not play Harding in football in its first two years. The first three meetings in the following three seasons were decidedly one-sided. WWR won all three, two of them by shutout, and had outscored Harding in those three games 64-6. By the fourth meeting in 1971, the two teams - players, fans, coaches, supporters, and alumni – openly did not like each other. As a freshman I got to go to the game, my first Raider game, because John DiGiacobbe's brother Dave had season tickets. One of the tickets was available because Dave's fiancé, a Harding grad, refused to sit with them among the Raider fans. She gladly went with them to every other game each year, and in case you were wondering, yes, they did eventually marry. Honestly, she was a sweetheart who taught at one of the elementary schools in Warren, but as a proud Panther, she simply drew the line at even a hint of supporting WWR.

There are a myriad of stories about the animosity between these two sides of the city; everything from the smirks of people who asked, because they *had* to know which school you went to, all the way to out and out fights, and most anything you can imagine in between. Once in my senior year, probably because a couple carloads of Harding students had cruised down our street and randomly egged cars and houses – and then actually threw them at me as I walked down the sidewalk - a few of us thought it would be fun to decorate up a car and drive around the east side in defiance. We did not counter-arm ourselves with eggs, but as it turned out, we didn't have to. It must have been a Friday, because we decided to "borrow" two sizable sections of the large banners that the cheerleading squad had taped up around the school for every football game which were painted on long paper scrolls about two feet wide. They must have worked hard at painting them, because there were new ones each week for each opponent. They would have been removed over the weekend anyway, and we reasoned that we could put them to good use in any case. So, we put one that read "West Side Pride" on one side of my mother's '69 Nova sedan, and another that read "Beat Harding" on the other side, both festooned in Raider gold, black, and white. As we headed east to cross the Summit Street bridge, we passed the house where several dozen fellow WWR students were hanging out, honked and were roundly cheered. A Reserve graduate lived in that house, which was essentially the first one west of the river and a little north of downtown. As a former and early Raider, he had an abundance of West Side Pride and each year during rivalry week went overboard with gold and white decorations, signs, and banners all over his property. He even used to set up a large teepee in the yard during football season. So every year, a considerable number of current and former WWR students gathered at his house each night to help fend off any problems.

We weren't across the river for more than a few minutes when we noticed another car speeding after us. They were hanging out their windows screaming at us, so we - just as Dirty Harry had recently reasoned - didn't figure they were out collecting for the Red Cross. I did my best Jim Rockford imitation and after using a few turns down a divided street we were afraid they had given up, so we baited them by slowing down and pumping the brakes. They came tearing after us again, at which point we zipped back westbound across the bridge, slowed down in front of the teepee house, yelling that the car behind us was from Harding and sped off. A mass of people immediately ran toward the street from the yard, bombarding the car that was chasing us, and collaterally a couple others, with wave upon wave of eggs. They were so inundated that the car swerved momentarily into oncoming traffic in the opposite lane and back, and had to turn on the windshield wipers in a vain attempt to clear the slime of eggs. Mission Accomplished. This episode is admittedly mild compared to the more prevalent actual fist fights and real property damage done by both sides that typically occurred that week each year.

A point that cannot be overstated is that the simple truth is that each side fervently disliked the other. The reasons for the animosity were many and extended well beyond a football game. Harding students referred to Reserve students as "river rats" - just one overt example of the condescension many east-siders felt. This was not just something people said in passing under their breath - which they also actually did. The term was painted on many of the corresponding signs that Harding's cheerleaders made, right there in plain view at Mollenkopf Stadium for everyone to see. Virtually everyone from Warren above voting age (which had been 21 until July of 1971) had gone to at some point, and most likely had graduated from Harding. Some of it undoubtedly had been just plain jealousy. A newly minted 1966 high school had considerably less wear and tear and - just guessing - a lot less asbestos to worry about. Many of WWR's teachers and staff had transferred from Harding, likely eager to start fresh in brand new surroundings. Some of them undoubtedly got a promotion they could not have otherwise received. So, in effect, building the new school also siphoned off some of the students' favorite or at least familiar faces. Realistically though, it would have been impractical to hit the ground running with grades 9-12 having only newly hired staff and faculty.

All of the 'old money', whatever there was of it, was on the east side. Doctors, lawyers, etc. invariably lived on the east side in the more established, proper neighborhoods, if they didn't live in other school districts just outside Warren. For that matter, two of Warren's three hospitals were sufficiently east of downtown and a third, but small Catholic hospital with limited facilities sat virtually just on the west bank of the river. Therefore, school board members and district supervisors were largely Harding grads or supporters. It's not hard to start feeling like second class citizens when everything is run by people much more closely associated with the other team. This clearly protracted all the way to the end of the rivalry. When the decision to re-integrate the schools was announced 15 or so years later, almost nothing was revealed publically about the criteria that were to be used in deciding which school would close. Well in advance of the decision announcement however was the oft-repeated and telling phrase,

"The decision will be irrevocable." Everyone knew what that meant: No one on the east side was going to send their kids to that swamp on the west side, no matter how much newer it was.

Emerging from this pretension of objectivity, the football game quickly developed into a living artifact of not just bragging rights, but status. It became a central focus and stayed that way for 22 years. In 1968, in the first meeting between the schools, Reserve won 14-6 on their way to a 9-1 win-loss record, while Harding finished at a respectable, but still deferential 8-2. In 1969, things did not get better for Harding. Reserve won 30-0 on the way to another 9-1 record. In 1970, Reserve won 20-0, and yet again went 9-1. Harding went 5-5 in both of these shutout years. This surely did not sit well with Warren's gentry, some of whom were likely responsible for hiring Tom Batta, a WGH graduate as Harding's new head coach in 1970. Batta's three year tenure as Harding's coach was bookended by 5-5 seasons, but it was that second campaign in 1971 that truly woke the echoes.

WWR entered the rival game in the fifth week of the season, with one loss. Just the previous week, they had played Dayton Kettering Alter. Down by a score of 20-14, WWR was driving steadily late in the game, when an offside penalty by one of the linemen derailed the comeback. With the penalty backing the team up and disrupting the team's momentum, they ran out of field position, and then ran out of time. Now we call the penalty 'false start', but the phrase used at the time, especially in high school football, was that the lineman had "jumped offside." I knew the guy who did it. He lived down the street and when he wasn't busy he would often shoot baskets or hang out with many of the kids of all ages who lived on the block, despite being larger than everyone. Feeling terrible about letting his teammates down wasn't the half of it. Another man just down the street had a daughter who had graduated from WWR just a couple years before, but other than that, had no real ongoing connection to the school. That did not stop him from relentlessly badgering the player about it. He would stop his car as he was going down the street if he saw the player and then start yelling at him from the car. He would walk to us from his house if he saw us talking to him or passing a ball with him. This continued for months, well after the football season had ended. It was not teasing; the man was clearly upset and voiced his displeasure repeatedly, and these were just the times I happened to be there to see it. To his credit, the player was stoic, he never got upset and he never walked away. The unfortunate part is that it is very likely that this was not the only person from whom he had to suffer abuse. He was a good football player and a guy you would want as a teammate. He had merely made what should otherwise have been an inconsequential mistake, had it not been made at the wrong time. The primary reason for the abuse was that everyone on both sides of the river wanted the fifth week rivalry game to be a battle of unbeaten teams, and now - the fall of 1971 - that wasn't going to happen.

These were formative times for the rivalry as yet another sold out Mollenkopf Stadium saw a hard fought battle between two good football teams. Both sides had talented players, but Harding arguably had more to fight for. By the time Harding reached the fifth game of the season, they had been battle tested against stalwart All American Conference opponents. This no doubt raised their confidence in hopes of avenging three straight years of losing the cross-town rivalry. Harding scored first on a pass play, but the first half ended with WWR up 8-7. The second half was a back-and-forth stalemate for both sides until Harding used another pass to set up a scoring drive with little more than three minutes to go in the game. The touchdown made the score 13-8, and Harding opted for insurance with a successful two-point conversion. The clock ran out on WWR's hopes of maintaining complete dominance of cross-town bragging rights and the game ended with Harding leading 15-8.

After five games, WWR was 3-2 and the prospect of having the worst season in five years did not sit well with West Siders. The team had not lost more than one game in a season since its very first campaign in 1966 when it ended the season 5-5. In retrospect, the mood around the school was considerably more subdued that would be experienced for the next few years, even though the team won out the second half of the schedule. After losing to Harding, Reserve narrowly edged East Liverpool by one point in the very next game, winning 9-8. The narrow victory appeared to energize the team, however, because after the win, they swept the remaining four games, three of them against conference rivals, by a combined score of 83-9. Following the season, uncertainty about the future clouded the mood even further when Head Coach Jim Hilles accepted an opportunity to coach at the college level. While the move in and of itself was necessarily neither a good or bad thing, the stars were about to align because of this decision.

The East Siders on the other hand, were truly in an ethereal Neverland. In 1971 for the first time ever, after 78 seasons of playing football, Harding had finished their season undefeated and untied. They had won ten games in the prior two seasons combined. In fact, the average number of wins per season over their existence up to that point was just under 5 games (4.98). But win out they did, including victories over several All American Conference rivals, and ultimately won the Associated Press Poll. At the time, that was as good as it got, but Harding did not win the last poll championship. The AP still declares a poll winner every year to this day. What they did win was the very last state championship in the absence of a valid playoff system.

It is now also known that the AP poll is as far as they could possibly have gone in 1971. Records indicate that in 1971 a test was performed by the Ohio High School Athletic Association of a ranking system by which playoffs might be used in high school football. At the end of the 1971 season, the test was declared a success, and the OHSAA decided to implement a playoff system in 1972, using the ranking system tested in the prior year. The final rankings for that test had Harding in second place in their region, and only the top teams in each of the four regions went to the playoffs. Reputation as a member of the storied All American Conference had garnered them the AP trophy, but finishing second using empirical rankings means they would not even have been in the playoffs.

3

SERENDIPITY

In many different contexts, I often recall the sage words of a colleague and mentor of mine, Professor George Bohlander. George has since retired as a distinguished full professor from Arizona State University, where he taught management and co-authored a widely-used textbook on human resource management that went well into the double-digit editions. He also used a grant he received for distinguished teaching specifically to create from scratch a business course in teams management, because he realized that conventional management teaching was focused on individuals, and was not necessarily the skillset needed to lead and manage a modern organization, whether in business or in sports. Now, most business schools do something similar; at the time, George's development of the coursework was on the cutting edge. The first time I heard him say it, we were watching the Chicago Cubs play a Spring Training game in Arizona, whereupon a base running mistake ended the inning. He turned to me and said resolutely, "A coach is only as good as his players."

One might assume that what he meant was that success as a coach was a crapshoot, that his or her success was only as good as the assemblage of individuals with which they were stuck. I knew when I first heard him say it however, that he meant considerably more than that. "A coach is only as good as his players" has symmetry; there are two sides to the equation. Coaching performance is revealed by how well the talents of the team's members are brought out and, even more importantly in a team sport, function in a coordinated manner. George's comment meant that the team hadn't been properly coached in base running - and very likely therefore, other aspects of performance as well. A *real* coach is a true leader who gets his team, individually and collectively, to realize its full potential. Ask an Oakland/Los Angeles/Oakland/Las Vegas Raider fan if, at any time since the late

80's, their team actually performed to the level of their potential or expectations. They have not, despite being cited repeatedly during this time period as one of the most talented NFL rosters for many of those years. The fact is that some people are better coaches. They see potential that most others miss. They know what to say, and how to best communicate it. They get everyone on the same page, working toward the same goal(s), even when their goals change. They demonstrate true leadership. When that happens, as it did at WWR in 1972, George's equation means 'a great team is the result of great coaching.'

* * * * *

When Joe Novak was hired as head football coach at Western Reserve in 1972, high expectations came with the job, but no one could have possibly realized how serendipitous the hiring was. Perhaps, it was obvious that he was simply the best candidate for the job. He had been an assistant coach under Jim Hilles who had just departed to the college coaching ranks, and therefore a known quantity, he had a Master's degree in Education (one of two coaches on the staff that had a Master's), and it could not have hurt that he was just so personable. Perhaps 'personable' isn't giving him enough credit. He was genuinely able to relate to anyone: age, race, gender... it absolutely did not matter. I saw this for myself over and over. He was a gifted public speaker, which is an incredibly valuable asset for someone taking this type of job, because a good coach also has to know what to say and how to say it, and this he did incredibly well. He would regularly be required to speak at meetings of the Booster Club, and the Quarterback Club, typically showing the game film and providing comments and modest levity. These were both community groups supporting WWR's athletics, with the latter more specifically supporting the football team. I believe they may have helped with things such as transportation, but I do know that one of these groups provided the football team's pre-game meals. His pre-game and half-time speeches were inspiring and to the point, and they were never the same - he did not repeat himself.

Coach Novak grew up not far away in Mentor, where he played in a high school football program that was steadily building a winning reputation. He went on to play college football at Miami University of Ohio, where Bo Schembechler was putting a winning stamp on Miami's football program before moving on to coach the University of Michigan. Miami was beginning to gain its reputation throughout the Midwest as "The Cradle of Coaches." Schembechler, along with notable coaches of the day Woody Hayes, Paul Brown, Sid Gillman, and Ara Parseghian, had incubated their coaching experiences at Miami and had carried success with them to major universities and in some cases on to the National Football League. Coach Novak knew the education, the coaching, and the professional training he had received as a player at Miami was unique, and he was not about to squander it. He knew the lay of the land in Northeast Ohio. He knew he was about to take over a football team with talent and potential. And, more than anything else, he knew that his job was to beat Harding.

Somewhat atypical in a state where football fans practically worshipped Ohio State's Woody Hayes and his fiery approach to coaching, Coach Novak didn't do a lot of yelling. Coaching high school students must come with frustrations from time to time, but whether it was planned or just his manner, he seemed to be more than happy to let the assistant coaches do the bulk of the yelling. Make no mistake however; when he did yell, you'd better be paying attention. His manner was even rarer in that he seldom, if ever, dressed down a player in front of his teammates. If things weren't going as they should in practices and he was getting frustrated, he'd blow the whistle, get right in the middle of scrimmage, and *emphatically* explain to everyone how the play is supposed to work. I recall though, that facilitating the timing and intricacies of the screen pass really tested his patience.

The rest of the coaching staff was essentially carried over from the previous season which provided continuity, along with a couple additions. At the varsity level, Dick Lascola and Bud Myers served as offensive and defensive coordinators respectively, and I doubt very much the school ever had two better coordinators. Harry Beers coached the offensive and defensive linemen, except for the defensive middle guards for some reason, who were Nick Earl's responsibility, along with the split ends, which were called "2-ends". Gilbert Jepson coached tight ends, while Harry Morrison and Joe Lukz designated as the Junior Varsity and sophomore teams coaches, with Pat Guliano, Steve Sisko, and Dave Campbell rounding out the staff. It was a fortunate mix of brains and brawn, with years of successful college playing and high school coaching behind them; the perfect coaching staff, ordained through serendipity. Raw talent can get you only so far. In 1972, WWR beat Harding, went undefeated, and won Ohio's first playoff championship largely because these men were great coaches.

Both Coach Beers and Coach Lukz liked to get into the mix. They had a very hands-on approach to coaching. Before and after a play in practice, it was not unusual to find one of them – without pads of course – demonstrating how to block, or fend off a block, or just plain lay someone out by doing it themselves. We were practicing place-kicking for field goals and extra points once, and I was in as the opposing defensive back trying to rush around the line to try to block the kick. After a couple tries, Coach Beers literally walked into the defense, grabbed the defensive end in front of me, replaced him with himself, and then turned to me and motioned behind his back for me to go behind him to the inside, not around the whole line. At the snap, Coach Beers slammed into the running back that was in a blocking stance at the end of the offensive line, in full helmet and pads, and not a small man by any measure, knocking him back and allowing me to slip inside the block on a direct route toward the kicked ball. Even though we all knew it was coming, we did it again, and then Coach Beers demonstrated to the back how best to block from that position and prevent someone from taking a shortcut inside.

Coach Beers was one of those men who looked as if he sneezed too hard, a full beard would pop out. He had a deep resonating voice almost stereotypical of a coach. At one point after a break, he surprised everyone by showing up with the most gnarly-thick Fu Manchu mustache anyone had ever seen *(remember, it was the 70s!)*. Everyone thought it was awesome, but it was also a short-lived expression. He shaved it down to a plain mustache after just a few days, then gone completely another day or two later claiming, "I kept getting food stuck in it." He always had a no-nonsense look to him, but the Fu-Manchu gave him the air of a Bond villain. If I had to guess, his look was probably scaring the crap out of his kids, and the wife set him straight. Interestingly, he was much more laid back as a teacher, particularly reveling in the attention from students that his all too brief fling with facial hair gave him.

Coach Lukz was from nearby Niles, Ohio, and had played football at Michigan, where Bo Schembechler was then the coach. I don't think it had been that long since he had graduated, because he really seemed to like getting in and demonstrating blocking or tackling techniques, and was always after us to do more reps lifting weights and the like. I recall more than once that he walked away from practice with a small cut or two bleeding from mixing it up with the guys in full pads. Coach Lukz and Coach Morrison were our sophomore team coaches, and Coach Morrison helped Coach Lascola with the defensive backfield when we were with the varsity team. Coach Morrison did not miss a thing on any play, and was quick to tell you and the three other guys that made a mistake what you did wrong, whether it was practice or a game (JV or Sophomore), but he also noticed when you did something particularly well and did not hesitate to tell you so. Coach Morrison also taught typing. I do not mean that he taught the keyboard - I mean he taught typing on old, extremely used manual typewriters. Everything was mechanical on these machines. They were far from new, probably made in the '50s, and very broken-in. So, for anyone who has never had the pleasure, this has nothing to do with gently pressing a plastic key on a computer keyboard. Every letter or symbol was on a separate metal arm that swung up and into a ribbon of ink, just above a sheet of paper. How well the letter or symbol looked on paper depended upon your finger strength and accuracy in pushing the keys with the correct and consistent force. I took the class not because I was in any way prescient in seeing the computer revolution ahead, but specifically because it took effort to type the keys correctly and evenly, and I wanted to strengthen my fingers to improve my hand coordination for catching a football. I think it actually helped, but to this day I hear Coach Morrison in my head drilling us, "F – F - J".

Bud Myers, the other coach with a Master's degree in Education, was a deep thinker. Sometimes I wondered about this because you could almost see the wheels turning as he took a moment before saying something after a play on the practice field. Eventually and because all high school coaches must also teach something, Coach Myers taught English and I had a term in creative writing with him. He would often muse about stuff that had nothing to do with English (or anything else) that he had been thinking about before class, which was right after his lunch. Usually it was just an odd comment, and then back to English writing, but one day he kept saying that he was 28 years old ... and that he wasn't so much worried about when he would die, as how. There wasn't a lot of class participation in the discussion that day. Even then I didn't regard 28 as old. Perhaps it was his birthday, and he was just wholly relieved to have beaten the "rock star curse" by getting past 27 to 28, I have no idea. But another time we had spent multiple class periods reading and discussing writing "styles", and our assignment was to write an essay entirely in a distinctive style. Owing to another English teacher who had told me in front of a different class that I had "a knack for sarcasm" (*perhaps you've noticed?*), I wrote a completely congruent and intentionally hilarious paper using almost nothing but one over-used cliché after another. It had an introduction, a body, and a conclusion, just like all high school English papers are supposed to have. When I got it back, all that Coach Myers had written on the bottom was "TOO TRITE" and given me a "C", apparently having once again been deep in thought about something else and completely forgotten the point of the assignment. From then on, I wrote every assignment conventionally regardless of his instructions and got my "A" for a final grade.

Dave Campbell was an enigma. He was also one of the coaches among several that did more than his share of yelling. Coach Campbell elevated yelling to an art form because that's just how he talked most of the time. On the practice field, in the classroom, it didn't matter. He coached the freshman teams year after year to a stellar record. He therefore might have made a good candidate for head coach, if it wasn't for the fact that, as rumor had it, he already had three jobs. I was told that in addition to being the driver's education teacher and football coach, he worked the graveyard shift at one of the local steel mills. I do not know this for a fact, but didn't doubt it. During summer conditioning drills and two-a-day practices, if you came across Coach Campbell during any break of any length, he was likely taking a nap anywhere he could find a spot. When he supervised us in the on-the-road driving hours as part of the driver's ed course, he would say, "Go out this-a-way" in a kind of deep southern-speak, lean his head against the window, and you would swear he had fallen asleep. Then, just about the time you were coming up on a traffic light, he'd suddenly raise his head and say, "Turn right here." We'd weave into a residential neighborhood, pick up his kids from where they were getting a music lesson or something along those lines, squeeze them into the back seat with the other student driver(s) and take the kids to some other lesson or activity. There, the kids would get out and he'd just say, "Head out this-a-way," point, and lean his head against the glass closing his eyes and off we would go on another Campbell family errand. The errands weren't any problem; we were getting our required on-the-road hours and could care less where we drove. We were just afraid he'd eventually genuinely fall asleep and one of his kids would be standing on a corner somewhere wondering where he was.

Aside from this, Dave Campbell knew how to coach, which his record alone proves. He was not my position coach, and I did not go out for football as a freshman, but he had a talent for motivating us, and he more than anyone ingrained into us that we had to work hard to beat Harding, and that beating Harding was all that mattered. Every time you rotated into a drill station that Coach Campbell was leading, we would do our full complement of whatever he had us do, and then he would have us do ten or twenty more "for Harding." Ask anyone: push-ups and grass drills are not fun, especially when you've just done forty. But Coach Campbell got us *wanting* to do ten more. We'd huddle up, chant - more than likely, "Beat Harding!" - and then go do ten more. Seriously, he's one of those guys of which it is said, "If he asked me to run through a brick wall, I would," even though I barely knew the man.

Make no mistake about it however, this was 1972, in the middle of Big Ten Country, and the mantra of successful football was 'three yards and a cloud of dust'. Woody Hayes, who was understandably big in Ohio at the time, is most often credited with the creation of that saying, and defending that philosophy by declaring, "Three things can happen when you throw the ball, and two of them are bad." Woody had very likely appropriated the latter tenet of mid-century football from a book by Darrell Royal, the head football coach at the University of Texas. Nevertheless, Woody raved it repeatedly on television over the years, and essentially got some if not all of the credit. No matter however, since at the time in high school, college, and even the NFL, the run dominated football. It's hard to believe especially with the excitement it brings to every football game at every level now, but at the time, passing the ball was an act of desperation, something you did when it was third down with more than four yards to go. This is because of course, the mantra 'three yards and a cloud of dust' implied that you would not get the first down by running the ball. Football was and is a macho sport, and there are not a lot of team sports left with the opportunity to show your manliness by bashing your head straight into your opponent over and over. Avoiding all that by passing a ball over top of everyone just seemed, well ... sissy ... as well as risky.

Need proof? Later that same season, the Miami Dolphins achieved the still one and only perfect season in the NFL, by completing a total of eight passes to win the Super Bowl. *Eight!* Nowadays, they complete eight passes in just one drive. Officially, the Dolphins' Bob Greise had only eleven passing attempts the entire game. As a note of karmic coincidence however, Greise would have been 9 for 12, had not a long pass to the aforementioned Warren native Paul Warfield been nullified by a penalty. As a member of the Dolphins, Warfield became the first Warren native and Harding graduate to win a Super Bowl ring and a second the following year, as well as the first in the Pro Football Hall of Fame.

WWR used an unbalanced line offense. To the left of the center were the backside guard, and next to him was the tight end, called the 8-end. To the right of the center was the strongside guard, inside tackle, outside tackle, and split out wide, the split end, or 2-end. The numbers referenced the running lane or position on the offensive line. Although we experimented with and had plays in the book for an I-formation backfield, the offense typically ran from a basic T-formation, although as coaches became more comfortable with our ability to run formations correctly, they mixed it up quite a bit. Behind the quarterback was the fullback, with a halfback both to his left and to his right. This meant that as a 2-end, my job (in practice, mostly) was to run as quickly as possible and block, headfirst, either the safety or the cornerback on defense. It got even more fun when they decided the 2-end could help the running game even more by cracking back on the defense's strong side linebacker. This was usually because they decided to run wide plays to the right. A crack back block would therefore shield the linebacker from pursuing the back who was running wide. Because blocking below the waist is illegal, this basically meant going helmet-to-helmet into a player who was often much bigger than you. Yes, today that would result in a penalty and even in high school, the average linebacker is bigger than the average wide receiver. I just thought it odd, as well as dangerous, because it wasn't two guys on the opposite side of the line not even two feet from each other at the snap of the ball. The 2-end had to gain steam by running in toward the line a few yards away to make the hit.

The defense was equally oriented toward 'cloud of dust' head-bashing. For whatever reason, WWR had eschewed the more mobile, versatile, and typical 4-3 defense, meaning your formation had four down linemen, and three upright linebackers - hence the name - behind them. WWR had been using and continued to use the 5-2 defense. The defense had five down linemen, including what we called a middle guard between the defensive tackles, and a left and right Linebacker. NFL teams of the day often had a player used similarly called a nose tackle, but whose position on the line varied and shifted considerably. It probably made sense, since most high school teams of the day ran the ball much more, you might as well have an extra body in the middle to close holes.

As a matter of interest, WWR's coaches only started modifying their defense a year later, and it was specifically because the team's upcoming opponent, Youngstown Cardinal Mooney, featured a highly talented running back named Ted Bell. The guy was being recruited by colleges all across the country, eventually choosing Michigan State. The long and the short of it is that essentially, they brought a safety close in on the defensive strong side and called him a "strong safety". It might have been a better idea to swap a safety for a third linebacker, but the coaches may have favored the slight speed advantage a defensive back might have had. For all intents and purposes, WWR was using a 5-3 with only three players in the defensive backfield, but then no one was particularly worried about a team that had Ted Bell passing the ball. The extra body on the line was there specifically to help defend against Bell, even if it just meant slowing him down a little, or making him shuffle/side-step until a teammate could tackle him. Among the strong safety's specific additional priorities - and I know this because I heard it explained when they introduced the defensive scheme to everyone in practice - was to hit Bell on every play (legally), whether he was the ball carrier or not. He usually was anyway. More on this later, but I'll just say it worked … the first time.

Preparations for an upcoming football season began in the winter. Well after the New Year, but often while there was still snow on the ground from time to time in Northeast Ohio, anyone who wished to go out for football and who wasn't busy with basketball, or baseball, or track, met together in the cafeteria after school hours. We were led by team captains Calvin Washington and Barry Simms in calisthenics. We did "Raider-jacks," jumping jacks where we spelled R-A-I-D-E-R-S as we jumped, did some stretching, and everyone's favorite: fingertip push-ups on the cafeteria floor. All of that pretty much just got our blood moving after a day of sitting around in classrooms. From there, we rotated in groups based on our class standing through different stations: free weights, universal gym, isometrics, and a fourth station that was partly determined by the weather and the ingenuity of the coaches. We were at each station about 20-30 minutes. For instance, some days we'd go to the basketball court if it wasn't in use, and run sprints, and other days we'd go outside and do them on the practice field no matter what the temperature. Sometimes we'd run the stairwells repeatedly, up and down, which was somewhat necessary because there were only three floors to the building. Every once in a while, we'd go to the gym and have very enthusiastic bouts of dodgeball … with multiple balls. I enjoyed these because I could catch the ball well, even if the volleyballs we used sometimes wobbled through the air like Phil Neikro's knuckleball. Catching a ball that was intended to hit and knock you out of the game, resulted in knocking the opponent who threw it out of the game and reinstating one of your own teammates who had already been knocked out of the game. When the teams started to dwindle because of hits, the coaches would blow a whistle and extend the boundaries for both sides, giving each opponent a very small nowhere-to-hide zone against each wall, along with a large overlapping mutual zone. It's a bit more challenging trying to catch a volley ball at close range while pinned against a wall when there are two or three of them being thrown at you at the same time by very large, very strong football players. The balls they threw didn't wobble; half the time you could hear them – ever so briefly - whizzing through the air. If the guys throwing were anywhere nearly accurate, I could probably catch one, but was hit by the other. If you just dodged them, the balls were thrown so hard, they bounced off the wall and quickly right back to them for another try at you.

Coaches awarded these McDonald's gift cards (front and back shown) for extra effort or winning a drill during spring conditioning. The McDonald's was within walking distance, across three sets of railroad tracks from the school, but for some reason, I never used these.

Every session we did what the coaches called isometric exercises, the most notable and regular of those being to strengthen the neck. Some took it a little more seriously than others, me included. For the record, I knowingly and willingly participated in the lead-with-your-head style of football. I also know for sure that I got my bell rung a few times as a direct result, for which I received the universal remedy of smelling salts. I was far from alone in that regard. We know better now, but it is not my intent to be critical of any coach, teammate, drill, technique, or football philosophy. This was undeniably the way football was taught and played in 1972, as well as long before and considerably long after. My opinion is that part of the lead-with-your-head issue stems from the fact that the modern football helmet, as it is designed, had and continues to have as much or more utility as a weapon as it does as a protective device. Fundamentally changing the helmet to function primarily as a protective device and reducing its usefulness as a weapon means changing the game as we know it however, so that is not going to happen.

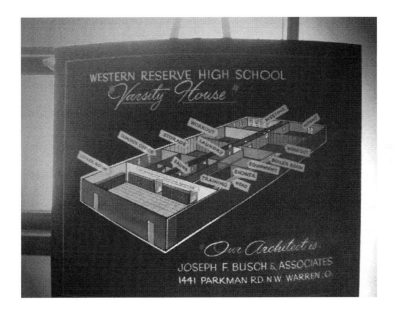

Picture of the conceptual drawing display for the Varsity House.

As a member of the team, among our other responsibilities specifically in early 1972 was to go out and sell tickets - not to the games - but to support the building of what was to be called the Varsity House. There was a definite need for updated facilities. The football locker room was in the bowels of the gymnasium. A heavy gray steel door led down a short flight of ten or twelve steps then turned left and then down another twelve. Ahead, another steel door opened to a concrete corridor, narrowed by the placement along its side of three or four free-weight stations for doing leg squats and overhead presses. By this point, the feel and the smell of the dank mustiness of six years of off-and-on intensive use became apparent. It was more or less the same as most team facilities, except that it was twelve feet or so below ground, encased on all sides by concrete block and walls of concrete, and had what must have been the minimum ventilation standard in 1966 when it was built. Those factors quite literally enhanced the athletic ambiance.

After the weight stations was a large heavy steel door behind which was some kind of industrial HVAC equipment or some other machinery necessary for a large public building. From time to time the noise from it was the very definition of cacophony and it echoed everywhere thanks to the concrete. The door was a large, industrial double-door, but one side had a few small dents in it that that seemed oddly shaped and out of place for some reason. At the door, another turn to the right led to a longer corridor with one or two more weight stations and two doors to the left; the first for the sophomore locker room, the second, well down the corridor, for the larger varsity locker room. Neither of the locker rooms were very big and everything had to be done in the allotted space. The sophomore locker room was barely big enough for twenty five guys with an adjacent small shower room. As it was, you pretty much had to take turns with the guy next to you getting your things in and out of your locker. Your helmet and pads fit in the locker, with some twisting and turning. The varsity locker room had a wide squared off U-shaped set of lockers and a universal gym taking up much of the space within the 'U'. Nobody wanted a locker in one of the corners, but some guys were stuck with them. Training tables for taping ankles and general training needs were in front of the sparse shower room. The coaches' (plural) office was just inside the door, but honestly, it was really a coach's (singular) office. I have no idea how all the staff fit their gear and change of clothes in there, it was so small. The uniforms, cleats, and equipment were stored upstairs in two utility closets using a pile-management system. Even if we had what you needed, good luck finding it. We would not see it until the following year, but by comparison the Varsity House would be clean, new, and spacious; comparatively a mansion. To help make it a reality however, we were assigned certain days and places spread out on the west side to try to sell tickets.

The off season training (as well as the ticket sales) went on for several weeks, all of which was done under the guidelines of the Ohio High School Athletic Association. The state's governing body prescribed rules and timelines for each sport, but also outlined when you could do, for instance, the off season conditioning, when you could do similar conditioning in the summer when school was out, and when specifically you could have students practicing football drills in full pads and helmets. One aspect of this that we particularly liked was that each year, the coach would bring a field official, someone who worked high school football games, to give us clarification on rules or rule changes and allowed us to ask him questions. Since it was this person's job to know the rules, it was very helpful, and one of those things you almost wished they'd have done a couple times a year. Coach Novak once had him clarify about the rules on a free ball, for instance when there's a fumble. This was deliberate because Coach wanted us to know that a free ball was just that. You could use your hands to grab the other team's player to push him out of the way to get to the ball, block him from getting to it, or in effect tackle him, as long as you didn't do anything otherwise illegal, such as clipping or unnecessary roughness. As an offensive lineman who was regularly prevented from using his hands, Larry Mallory could not contain himself at this news. With a joyous smile, he kept asking the official a series of questions – "So I can push another guy away to get to the ball?" "Yes." "I can grab him and push him out the way?" "Yes." And so on. Grinning from ear to ear, he also knew it applied on special teams: kickoffs, punts touched by the other team, and blocked kicks. Admittedly, these are typically a very small portion of a game, but a fumble could potentially happen at any moment. Larry had an easy going I'm-just-here-to-kick-some-butt-and-have-some-fun manner to him, and he *really* loved it when someone got laid out by a solid hit or tackle in practice. Most guys just did what they were told. But Larry knew what his job was on every play and, even though he was a lineman, he pretty much knew what everyone else should be doing because he knew what the play was designed to do. This became apparent when he once succinctly and effectively dressed down one of our quarterbacks about a play that we did not often use. There was no yelling, no finger pointing. Larry told him the way it was, the QB knew he was right, and then Larry walked away. He was a very good football player, partly from his athletic talent and partly because when it came specifically to football, he was very smart.

The summer football conditioning amid the glorious heat and humidity of northeast Ohio was aptly called "Tuffy." In July, long before we were allowed to put on pads and helmets, we met regularly for conditioning drills on the practice fields. Day after day we did 40 yard wind sprints, grass drills, and agility drills, all to increase everyone's stamina. We rotated through stations once again, which always included the free weights and the universal gym downstairs. It was a lot cooler inside at the weight stations, but we looked forward to rotating outside to the heat just for the fresh air. Again, there was not a lot of ventilation down there. If it was pouring down rain, that was even more preferable. The rain cooled you off, even if it did make some drills sloppier. So, everything's wet and muddy ... guaranteed we would do grass drills. That's where we form a large circle facing each other and while running in place, the coaches call out, sometimes a number to count them out and sometimes just "DOWN!," at which time you drop face down on the ground, push yourself back up and continue running in place, all in one quick motion. After a dozen or so, somebody inevitably was dragging and missed the drop and push. That would usually cost us an additional ten; each and every one of which we would count off his name, "ONE because of (name)!", ""TWO because of (name)!" and so on. It really pissed us off when two or three different guys missed a drill, and even more so when that happened later during full uniform practices when fatigue invariably caused it.

Most of these days blurred one into the other, but one or two things stuck in my memory. As summer dragged on and it got even hotter, someone arranged to give out watermelon slices to everyone at the conclusion of practice. I don't know if it was the coaches or perhaps the quarterback club, but it was a welcome and rare treat, usually only a time or two each summer. A third possibility is that it may have been some of the people from the community on the sides of the fields watching and encouraging us. Some were retired, some were just interested. Mr. Buffone, who lived across the street and a couple houses away from me, walked the few blocks and was at Tuffy almost every day. He took considerable interest in the team, and would occasionally ask me, "What was that about?" regarding this or that, or some more specific question about what we had done or why, later when I would see him on our block. His sons had gone to Reserve a couple years earlier but to my knowledge did not play football. There was a rumor that his family was in some way related to Doug Buffone, one of the Chicago Bears' other linebackers at the time who toiled in the shadow of the legendary Dick Butkus, but it was likely just one of those rumors that started because of his name. I think he was just interested in our team and wanted to be supportive. It may have been some of the observers like him that decided to get a bunch of watermelons from time to time, I really don't know.

Each session, regardless of which station you had begun with, everyone met outside for one or another drill and then we closed with a piggyback drill. The coaches formed a kind of human barrier about ten yards square on the practice field using cones and themselves to firm up the corners, and everyone paired up and had to run around the entire square in mass with the other person on your back. As might be expected, jostling ensued by other pairs of players, and by the coaches, who pushed out the pairs closest to the square, especially as guys rounded the corners. If you fell off or fell down, you had to get back on and finish. With all the jostling, there was a lot of falling. That was only half my problem however. New to the drill as I was, I was surprised when the second it was announced, Jim King turned to me and said, "Hop on." Jim King was our starting fullback and he was listed in the program at 175 lbs., surely he was at least that. I was neither of these things. So, the veteran he was, he looked for the first thin guy he could find. More serendipity: I happened to be standing next to him. I actually didn't mind, I figured it was good for me when we swapped and I had to carry him. We always made it, but definitely slower with him on my back. I say always, because we looked for each other and paired up pretty much each time the drill was about to start. Nobody wanted to be an odd man out without a partner. If you were, Coach Lukz was eager to hop on your back so you didn't miss out. So, let's say you have a choice of quickly pairing up with a teammate or have Coach Lukz, a guy who looked like he could still be the University of Michigan lineman he had recently been, literally riding you. No contest.

Another time we were finishing our next to last station lifting weights downstairs when Coach Campbell told us "Time to go" but as we climbed the stairs and exited the building, he realized we were early and needed to keep us busy. So he improvised. The exit door led out to concrete sidewalks that extended 30 or 40 feet in the direction of the practice fields. So, in his deep resonating voice and distinctive cadence, he yelled, "I WANT YOU...TO RUN DOWN TO THE END OF THIS HERE CON-CREEK...YELLIN' ALL THE WAY...FIGHTIN' RAIDER ... ... AND WHEN YOU GET TO THE END...DO A SOMERSAULT IN THE GRASS!" Then, "Line up!" and very quickly, "DOWN! SET! DOWN! SET! DOWN! SET!" as one by one in a line, we each dropped to a three-point stance on "Down" and took off yelling "Fighting Raider" at "Set" while the next person jumped in line behind you. If Coach Campbell improvising a time-filler at the top of his lungs wasn't funny enough, many of the attempts at somersaults were. We were definitely not a gymnastics team. At the end of the sidewalk to the left was a small parking lot, so had he thought a bit longer about it than he did, Coach Campbell might have told us to go pick up a car. And we probably would have tried it. So, we got off lucky just doing somersaults. As it turns out, a car actually did get picked up a few weeks later.

After months of conditioning, we prepared to transition to putting on actual pads and practicing real football. In the last few days, we went to the gym where among several large boxes or spread along the gym floor were our football helmets - reconditioned, repainted, and ready for use – along with football cleats. There were a variety of helmet styles, sizes, and already-attached facemasks which could be swapped easily. Some guys immediately looked for the few modern (for the day) air helmets, which could be form-fitted by adjusting the amount of air in several pockets or sleeves inside the helmet using needle valves on the outside. They tended to be more comfortable, and were regarded as a superior type of helmet. They probably were, because a year later they specifically held one out to give to one specific freshman, which was very unusual at the time. Most of our helmets were full of fairly stiff padding that corresponded to your hat size, which was embossed on the back of the helmet, and that's where the majority of us were finding one that fit. The air helmets were undoubtedly more expensive, which was all the more unusual to have given one specifically to a freshman, so there must have been some reason to do so.

There were also a few "water helmets", which had strong bladders of connecting segments of liquid inside so that upon impact, the liquid would slosh through connections in the segments, providing a cushioning effect. I tried one briefly, but found that not only were they heavy, the fluid did not just immediately flow back into the segment it came from. So, upon any impact from a blocking drill, tackling, etc., which was expected to be done using your helmet, the fluid quickly flushed away from the segment at point of impact, and only very gradually seeped back. So if you were in drills having repeated contact, the amount of fluid cushioning at the point of impact was less and less. There'd be plenty of fluid oozing its way to the segments in the back of your head, for all the good that would do you. But some guys loved them. Larry Rihel took the water bladder out and put it in the refrigerator or freezer before games early in the season when it was still very warm, and ... well, for later games too. You couldn't do that, nor would you have any reason to, with any of our other helmets. In any case, we were to wear the helmets to get used to wearing them because, as was the training technique of the time, you couldn't take your helmet off once practice started. Which was all the more reason to get the best one that you could find, and that fit you as well as possible.

With our entire focus on beating one team, we could not have imagined where all that preparation was going to take us.

4

HARBIN

WWR's team name and mascot – Raiders - was not the bruising eye-patched invader that still adorns Las Vegas's NFL team helmets. WWR's Raiders were intended to harken to an historical aspect of the school's name: the Western Reserve. The Native American warrior that served as the embodiment of WWR Raider Pride echoed the proverbial untamed wilderness that was the school's namesake. A stoic profile view of this Native American served as reference point and identity for the Warren Western Reserve Raiders. WWR's black football helmets were adorned with a gold and white feathered spear on both sides. A student mascot dressed head-to-toe in buckskin, with a large flowing headdress and carrying a real feathered spear appeared at every football game, pep rally, and other student activities. Before the start of football games, the marching band would play a now arguably inappropriate drumbeat to which the mascot would dance out and throw the spear into the air toward midfield. Tradition declared that if the spear stuck, the Raiders would win the game. Of course, the spear was weighted on the end, making it easier to give fans something else to cheer.

Today, many of the traditions of the school would be regarded as politically incorrect, if not blatantly offensive. Charlene Teters, a Native American former graduate student at the University of Illinois is generally credited with starting the national movement to stop using Native images as mascots. She may not have actually started it, but she certainly helped bring the issue to national attention. Yet there were many universities that had already begun renaming their teams before anyone had heard of her. Her initial objections started when she attended a University of Illinois basketball game and was appalled to see a lily-white student in full buckskin, headdress, and regalia dancing an incongruous modern interpretive dance all around the basketball court;

activities which she considered offensive and mocking. One cannot but imagine what Teters would have thought of WWR's Raider prancing about a football field and throwing a real spear. I actually do understand her specific objections to Chief Illiniwek, as he was called until the school decided in 2007 that enough was enough. But, others took the headway that her specific objection was making and painted it with a broad brush. So I have to ask ... being Irish, should I be offended by the fisticuffed leprechaun of Notre Dame's "Fightin' Irish"? The Cleveland "Indians" are no more, even though Teters herself had stated plainly that she had no objection to a caricature.[8] *(Long Live the Guardians!)* Still, today there remains more than enough offensive behavior within Major League Baseball by the Atlanta Braves and their fans for those so inclined to pursue the issue.

In 1973, in connection with building the Varsity House, a sizable winged totem pole was also built behind the facility. No one seemed to question why Native Americans from northeast Ohio would have a totem pole. I'm a little surprised that no one ever tried to deface it, in the manner of a competitive rivalry like Army and Navy, each of which had tried to kidnap the other's mascot over the years. I am certain however that no one regarded it as offensive at the time. Perhaps even worse, most everyone paid no notice to it at all. It was located in a lonely spot behind a building near the edge of the property, and the only times it served any purpose whatsoever was when for warm-up or warm-down, the coaches had us all run to it, around it, and back to wherever we were on the practice fields.

[8] See Rosenstein, J. (1997). *In Whose Honor?*

The totem pole behind the Varsity House.

That's really not the half of it, though. WWR's football team called its defensive unit the Blood Defense. Seemingly in character and not in and of itself offensive, but yet – to this day I do not understand how this ever happened – WWR's offense was called the Blitzkrieg Offense. This would create social media frenzy today, and it's a little confusing how it happened at all when the school opened, just twenty years after World War II ended. If your history is rusty, "Blitzkrieg" was a Nazi term for their highly coordinated, highly effective military attacks, e.g. invading Poland[9]. This would not be unlike your local high school football team cheering on their Al-Qaeda or Taliban offense today. Maybe people did have second thoughts about it however, because invariably the fans' cheers were shortened to "Go Blitz" (which then could be confused with the defensive maneuver of the same name) and nearly all printed references to it, such as the yearbook and the local newspaper, simply said "Blitz Offense."

---

[9] Coincidence: Poland was also the name of a suburb of Youngstown with its own high school. Fortunately, we did not play the Bulldogs in football.

Interestingly, although modified from WWR's profile image, the re-integrated Harding team remains the Raiders. And, in case you're wondering, I kind of like that leprechaun.

* * * * *

A better system to determine the Ohio's high school football champion had been proposed as long ago as 1960. A writer for Cleveland's *Plain Dealer* named Ed Chay suggested in his column that the state should create a system, based on points, to delineate the top ten teams. His suggestion, despite the *Plain Dealer*'s wide readership fell on apparent deaf ears (*or is that blind eyes?*). It took another ten years until a cash register repairman from Wickliffe presented a practical idea. Jack Harbin's relevance to this part of Ohio's history was two-fold; he volunteered as an assistant football coach at Wickliffe's high school and more importantly to history, was a math enthusiast. Harbin believed that a playoff system was not only needed, but possible.

Harbin felt that smaller schools, like his own Wickliffe, were not appreciated enough by the AP and UPI poll makers. Like everyone else in the state, he also knew that the poll system had effectively devolved into a rote exercise of reputation or popularity, exactly like picking the Super Bowl MVP persists to this day. He proposed what is effectively a strength-of-schedule point system based solely on whether a team wins, loses, or ties each opponent. Dan Coughlin, another *Plain Dealer* sports writer, called Harbin's system a "geometric pyramid." This tautological phrase (*Like "round circle" - Do you know any other kind?*) neither properly describes it, nor helps people understand it, but if it helps one conceptualize it as a model, so be it. Teams are awarded first-level points for games they win or tie and second level points for games those defeated opponents win. Thus, point totals for a school that has beaten good teams who were otherwise winning the remaining games on their schedules can rise significantly week-to-week. From the beginning, third level points were calculated as well, whereby points were earned from the defeated opponents of the second level teams. As you can imagine, points can accumulate quickly by the time third level points are earned. Presumably for the test season of 1971, but definitely for the ranking system actually used in 1972 and 1973, the third level points were used to determine the playoff entrant in each of four regions. Thereafter, starting in 1974, third level points were to be used only as a tie-breaker, but curiously are not reported in OHSAA records from that point forward. The first notation made of any tie within archival rankings was not until 1986.

There was and there remains no provision in the OHSAA system for total yards, or total points for, or total points against as either supplemental measures or tie breakers as is done for the NFL playoffs. The algorithm which precisely determines the point values assigned at each level initially seemed to remain a high level state secret on par with Coca-Cola's secret formula, but the fact is that the precise calculations are available with excellent examples on the Ohio High School Athletic Association's website. Obviously this was not the case at its inception during the 1970s. From a practical standpoint, and as a matter of historical fact, all any team could hope to do was win every game they played, and perhaps that was the idea from the beginning. I know for certain that despite finishing with a perfect 10-0 regular season record in both 1972 and 1973, and despite their best efforts at trying to calculate point totals themselves, our coaches did not know whether we were in the playoffs or not until they got a call from state officials.

Another former academic colleague of mine examined organizational communication and was insistent that communication works best when you, "Either tell them everything, or tell them nothing." The gray area in between opens the door for speculation on the road to fear and false rumor. Newspaper sportswriters of the day were likely never very clear in the early years of Ohio's playoffs on exactly how the point system worked, and some details were likely omitted in reporting it to the public. So, as you might expect given some limits on information and comprehension, matters were complicated by a rumor that had spread like wildfire on the west side leading into the final game of the season with Lorain Southview. Lorain was perennially bad at football (apologies to Lorain, but it was simply the truth at that point in time), and because, as a member of our North East Ohio Conference, they had thus lost to every conference opponent that we had already beaten earlier in the season. Follow the logic here as I try to connect the dots. Owing to the fact that almost no one in 1972 genuinely understood how points were assigned to teams for the playoffs, people started insisting that WWR should deliberately lose to Lorain because, A) Lorain would get all of our points which would mean, B) All the other conference teams that we had beaten - and which had beaten Lorain - would get Lorain's surge in points and thus, C) Because we had already beaten all of those teams, our point total would potentially be more if we lost the final game than if we won. In other words, our sizable number of points would circle back to us. Back to reality: that wasn't going to happen. I felt sorry for Coach Novak, who had to address the "plan" repeatedly. I heard him say multiple times, "That's not how it works," not just to individuals, but also when the question was asked at the Quarterback Club meeting. Whether he knew that or not didn't matter, because he lived and imbued into us a sense of sportsmanship. We would play every game to win and whatever happens, so be it. I found it hard to believe, even as a teenager that a sponsor would suggest that we lose a game, but some of the club may also have confused the points that the OHSAA awarded with the cumulative points that had been scored in the games. In any case, Novak's moral compass direction was: you win every game possible, because the playoff invitation is neither up to you nor under your control.

As an academic researcher, I can say for certain that the more reliable and accurate information that you have and use, the better results you will have. Because the objective all along was to determine which teams had the best record against the best teams, this would best be accomplished by including third level points in the calculation. This is a very definition of strength-of-schedule. Since A) there were no issues with ties for the first two seasons, and B) the information was and still is compiled and processed each week, it remains a question as to why OHSAA would stop using the third level points in 1974 after only two years. Statistically speaking in fact, doing so means that determination of each region's winner - and therefore playoff entrant - unquestionably becomes less accurate. Using them in the total point count for the first two years may have been more precise measures, but that inconsistency also meant that in at least two cases in the first two seasons, a team with *fewer* first and second level total points finished first and entered the playoffs ahead of teams with *more* first and second level points. The third level points put these teams ahead in a complete absence of any tie. This is exactly what should have happened.

The touchstone of a strength-of-schedule system is that while your overall record is somewhat important, more relevant is the quality of the teams that you beat. It means, for instance, that a good team (by its record) could be left out of the playoffs by a not-quite-as-good team that played and beat eight or nine other stronger teams. It's at least theoretically possible. In fact, it's more than theoretically possible, and the OHSAA proved it themselves.

In 1986, Delphos Jefferson and Tiffin Calvert tied for the Region 18 final qualifying position. A notice prefacing the archival final 1986 computer rankings stated that the tie-breaking system was used, "In case of a tie in any region for fourth qualifying team, the team schedules of the tied teams shall be computed using the third level of competition to break the tie."[10] The regulation applies across the board to any tie at any level. But this notation was made to the notice in 1986, where the third level points didn't merely break the first-ever tie. In 1986, they broke that tie of first and second level totals by proving that Tiffin had played - and beaten - better opponents. Tiffin and Delphos were tied at 59 points until third level points showed that the opponents of the teams that Tiffin played were considerably better. Tiffin entered

[10] OHSAA addendum Notice dated November 4, 1986, (https://www.ohsaa.org/Portals/0/Sports/Football/pastresults/final-cpu-rankings/1986.pdf)

the tournament with 172.9444 points leaving Delphos out with only 118. If Tiffin and Delphos were truly equal, the third level points should have merely given one of them the edge. The OHSAA thus proved that third level points are vital to determining which teams had the best record against the best teams, but the preface to the 1986 rankings more than implies that, since 1974, they don't even bother to calculate them unless necessary.

But there was Jack Harbin, crunching numbers from schools all over Ohio and its surrounding states week after week – recording it all by paper and pencil, using many of Ohio's newspapers as reference. To restate emphatically: A) He started doing this in the early 1960s and B) There were no computers. In fact, when Harbin finally presented his proposal to the Ohio High School Athletic Association in 1970, their so-called expert said it couldn't be done without a computer. For 1970, this is an interesting and telling comment on Harbin's comprehensiveness and dedication, because Harbin had in fact been doing it. By hand. For years. After plodding along with his idea for a couple seasons, in 1966 Harbin managed to convince Dan Coughlin to print his rankings in the *Plain Dealer* sports section each week of the season. In his book, *Crazy, With the Papers to Prove It*, Coughlin gives credit to Harbin in one of the many brief stories of Ohio sports therein. However, a significant amount of indebtedness should be given to Coughlin himself for appreciating and believing in Harbin's calculations and intentions and then providing or allowing him space in the paper. It must have been a bold move to print the rankings of essentially an unknown amateur in Ohio's largest newspaper. Although there certainly appeared to have been no one else stepping up to the plate to propose or examine the mathematics involved. In fact, the math wasn't any real problem; the problem was getting the correct information (e.g. which teams played, who won, etc.) in a timely manner in the pre-internet days of the 1960s and 70s that resulted in most of the effort.

In 1970, four years after first printing his rankings in the *Plain Dealer*, Harbin was invited, however reluctantly one must assume, to present his system to the OHSAA. Having proven the math behind his ranking system and the fact that it could be reasonably done by hand, the OHSAA agreed to test Harbin's system the following football season in 1971, but by actually using a computer. Few details or criteria seem to be available, but the test was declared a success, and both Harbin's ranking system and his playoff recommendations were adopted for the 1972 football season. For practical reasons, Harbin divided the state's high schools into four regions in each of three classes, based on enrollment. The four regions meant there were four teams, allowing for a semi-final game, followed by a championship game in each of the three classes. Within Class AAA were the larger schools, the ones that had been winning the AP writers' poll year in and year out, but an important aspect was that smaller schools with traditionally good programs could now compete among their peers within Class A and AA for a real championship. Before this, a school like Wickliffe or Mentor with its strong program could never have feasibly won an AP poll championship, because the school simply wasn't big enough and because it was never given the notoriety that other schools took for granted. With the poll system invariably favoring the larger and well known schools (i.e. Class AAA), small schools never had a chance; no matter how good they were. Jack Harbin's system came about because favoritism and familiarity severely restricted opportunity. This is the inherent problem with polls, and it is not restricted to high school. Before a playoff system was introduced in college football, writers and other so-called experts debated the rankings and the crowning of a national champion nearly every year. In fact even with it, they still debate it, because the playoff field remains small and discounts smaller schools with up and coming programs.

When the OHSAA decided to adopt his system, they asked Harbin what he wanted for his efforts. Harbin literally had years invested in his idea, but asked only to have his name put on the ratings as a simple recognition of his efforts. Thus was called the

Harbin Rating System ... up to and until 1984, whereupon it was summarily dropped for reasons unknown. The OHSAA website provides the digitized versions of the final computer rankings printout for every season since they began in 1972. His name disappears after 1984. This represents a massive disservice to someone who knew the system was flawed, set about to fix it, and showed them how to do it. Whatever modifications have occurred to the system over the years, it is still based on Jack Harbin's paper and pencil calculations that he began 60 years ago, and which have been adopted by other states all over the country. His memory and his significance deserve better. A great many young men across the country, not just in Ohio, have Jack Harbin to thank for the championship trophy or ring that they might never even have been given an opportunity to win.

But a playoff system did not spell the death knell of the polls. The UPI continued for several years before bowing out. The AP continues to publish a poll after about the fifth week each week of the season and declare a champion at the close of the regular season, despite that a proven, empirically valid system of playoffs has been in place for fifty years. On one hand, some might argue this to be a good thing. It's another "championship", however much "mythical", that can be claimed. On the other hand, it was the favoritism and biases of such a poll that Jack Harbin wanted to eliminate and quite effectively succeeded in doing. By providing what is essentially a consolation prize based on reputation instead of proving you were the best on the field seems to do more harm than good. It's akin to continuing to drive a horse and buggy to prove it can still be done, or worse, because a small cloistered and elite group of people insist it's the best way to do things, even as an electric sports car zooms past. It's an abject impossibility that AP voters could possibly be familiar with every high school team in the state, *or even just every one of the teams on which they vote*. That's not to say the AP hasn't learned from the new system. In the 27 years between 1946 when the AP began awarding the state's mythical championship and 1972 when the playoffs began,

Massillon "won" 13 times, effectively, half of them. The last time they were awarded the AP trophy was 1972, the year the playoffs started, and even that was days *before* a playoff game had ever been played in Ohio. The AP still today declares a champion after the final games of the regular season - before any playoff games begin.

In the fifty years since: Massillon has never won the AP poll or the playoff championship. At least the playoffs managed to broaden the AP's attention span. Playoffs have done nothing to improve the AP's accuracy, however. In the fifty years of high school playoffs for Class AAA or Division 1 high schools, The AP poll champion has matched the playoff champion in only 17 years of the fifty, or about once every three years. It took the pollsters five years to match the first playoff champion correctly. The focus of this discussion is that of Class AAA or what would later become Division 1 schools, which are the largest in terms of enrollment and the schools with which, presumably, AP writers should be most familiar.

More specifically and relevant to the rivalry between Warren's schools and as a matter of interest, if the Harbin ranking system had been implemented rather than just tested in 1971, Harding would not have been champion. This is because they would not have been in the state playoffs associated with the rankings, although it is at least possible that the AP poll would still have declared Harding champs. The final, unused test rankings in 1971 had Parma scoring at the top of Region 1, the same region which included Warren. Harding, which was second on the list, would therefore not have been in the playoffs, if they had occurred[11].

---

[11] Ruman, Steve, Harbin's Ratings Changed Ohio Football, *Youngstown Vindicator*, Nov.9, 2018.

	OHSAA 1971 TEST RANKINGS		
WEEK 10	CLASS AAA		REGION 1
RANK	CITY - HIGH SCHOOL NAME		
1	PARMA		
2	WARREN HARDING		
3	MENTOR		
4	LAKEWOOD ST. EDWARD		
5	MAYFIELD HEIGHTS		

Reproduction of the test of Harbin's Rankings for 1971 in Region 1.

* * * * *

Conceptually, Harbin's ranking is a relatively straightforward three-step system to determine how "good" a team is, based solely on wins and losses. In terms of playoff selection: which team ranks the best against the best opponents (within each region)? To do this requires an examination of *both* how good a team (Team A) and how good Team A's opponents are. To do the latter requires an examination of the opponents of Team A's opponents. This is because a win-loss record by itself tells very little about any given team. If a mediocre team plays mainly within a bad conference, their subsequent good win-loss record, by itself, provides a deceptively positive impression. Conversely, if a team plays in a highly competitive conference, a seemingly mediocre record provides a deceptively negative impression. There's evidence this deception happens and that win-loss record alone doesn't tell the story.

It requires a three-step process. First, to determine how good Team A is, examine Team A's win-loss record. Unfortunately, this tells you very little, because you don't know how good the ten teams were that they played. Second, you have to examine the record of each of the teams that Team A played. Again, the record itself tells you next to nothing. To know how good the ten teams that Team A played were, in order to ultimately rank how good Team A was, you must examine the teams their opponents played. This requires a third step. The third level records provide an indication of how good the ten teams that Team A played are, something that second level win-loss records alone do not. These three steps provide the information necessary to determine the ranking of any one team. The third level tie-breaker points for Tiffin in 1986 prove this.

Additional evidence of third level points indicating as to how good were a team's opponents occurred early on, in 1973. Harding, playing against storied rivals in the All-American Conference, finished eighth in OHSAA Region 1 (out of 69 teams), despite having a very modest 6-4 record. Such a record should have placed them much closer to the middle of the rankings. Their eighth place ranking demonstrated that, despite what must have been a disappointing season, they had played and had some success against a strong schedule of opponents. It's also why, even from the beginning, sports writers like Dan Coughlin recognized the final three-level rankings as a "progression."

Any further, for example a fourth level, would result in what is referred to as diminishing marginal returns as well as go well beyond the objective of determining an individual team ranking, and with considerably more work involved. A secondary and real problem is an inherent intercorrelation of data. Effectively, at a fourth level, the number of games necessary to examine becomes exceedingly large and many of these teams will have played each other with widely varying results. Good teams will have lost to teams that in turn lost to teams with apparently poor records, and every other combination possible of wins, losses and ties between large numbers of teams. The net result essentially, is that the information quickly begins to contradict itself, or effectively, cancel itself out.

After years of thankless and selfless laboring, there would be playoffs in Ohio to determine the state's football champion in 1972. The result of Harbin's efforts was a framework that has endured for fifty years - so successful that it has been adopted by other states. The playoff framework was modified over the years, including expansion in 1980 from three Classes (AAA, AA, A) to five Divisions (I-V). Regional playoffs were also eventually added.

In the beginning however, the four highest ranked teams in each of the four regions (in each Class) played in the two semi-final games. Typically it was the Region 1 winner playing Region 2, and Region 3 playing Region 4 in the semi-finals. After which, the winners of those two games played in the final game for the state championship.

Jack Harbin had done it. It was not his sole motivation, but a footnote to this accomplishment is that it was not until 1985 that Harbin's Wickliffe High School Blue Devils first qualified for the expanded state tournament. In the fifty years of Ohio football playoffs, they have appeared ten times.

5

PERFECT

One aspect to this football team that was hard to grasp was the turnover. There were two WWR team pictures taken in 1972. The first picture, at the beginning of the season, with all of the seniors and juniors in black jerseys - a typical varsity team photo - had 64 players in it. The second picture, taken in white jerseys after the regular season and just before the first playoff game had the seniors, juniors, and sophomores in it. Our sophomore team had its season cancelled after one game, then resumed, then cancelled for good. More on that later, but its members, such as myself, had effectively been drafted onto the varsity. We certainly earned our keep as practice dummies and scout team players during the season. That second photo had 72 players in it, 19 of which were sophomores. Three guys, sophomores Joe O'Grady, Bill Ritter, and Bob Kascsak, missed the photo session that day for some reason, so there should have been 75 in the second picture[12]. Everyone that was still on the team, except Joe, Bill, and Bob, is in that photo. If we added 22 sophomores to the pre-season varsity photo, the second picture should have had 86 players in it, but there were only 72 with three being absent.

There were always a few people who quit after a few two-a-day sessions in the summer, or at some time before they ended. But this seems an unusually high number, especially because the first photo is taken when the season is about to start. The really not-fun part is over with, and … they quit a winning team. In fact, the following year and probably because of the success we had in 1972, a lot of new guys were there at the start of two-a-days, but it didn't take long before almost all of them, except for a couple, were gone.

---

[12] Matt Miller being injured and unavailable made a total of 76 at season's end.

At the start of two-a-days in 1972, all anyone on our team cared about was beating Harding. The coaches were undoubtedly aware of the fact that the state had created a playoff system, but it was not mentioned. What was mentioned was that everyone had to work harder because the team had one goal: Beat Harding. Losing to them, which had occurred for the very first time the year before, was unacceptable. This was reinforced to us every day, every practice, twice a day ... and even before that.

Just before two-a-days started after a weekend break, we picked up the rest of our equipment: shoulder pads, pants and padding, hip pads, practice jersey, mouth piece, shimmel shirt, socks, etc. After we sorted out what we wanted or what fit, we were to take the gear down to the appropriate locker room and choose a locker. Taking my gear to the sophomore locker room, I picked what was probably the same locker that I had been using during spring conditioning and then peeked through the adjoining door into the varsity locker room. Both locker rooms had been cleaned but something looked different in the varsity room. Curiously, people were standing there looking at the floor. The universal gym had been moved and everywhere within the "U" of lockers the floor had been newly painted black. In the middle of the floor in the yellow that we called gold, in very big block letters was painted **VARSITY FOOTBALL**. Centered below that in very big - very red - letters was **15-8**.

* * * * *

Practice makes perfect. But only if you do it right. Two-a-days only partly describes our activities. Generally, there was a morning practice, followed by a 90-120 minute lunch break, followed by classroom instruction, according to your position. There, each play in the playbook and your specific position responsibilities were explained, and we went through it page-by-page. After another shorter break, we started afternoon practice, often throughout the heat of the afternoon. At other times, the classroom periods were used for additional weight lifting or in some cases, therapeutic treatments for the inevitable bumps and bruises. I recall only one time that afternoon practice was cancelled and that was because it was forecast to be above 100 degrees that day. On the 90+ degree days we were given either or both: salt pills or a Kool-Aid flavored drink concocted by coaches. They both gave you a headache, especially when they insisted you take several of the pills, but the Kool-aid was just plain horrible. They knew we would drink it however because there was nothing else. We had no hoses running out to portable drinking fountains or anything resembling what is commonplace now, so a line formed at the fountains inside when practice ended. I am not sure what else was in the drink because although they wouldn't say what, they did say they had put several things in it. It was definitely salty and although I did not taste it for all the salt, also suspect there was sugar in it for energy. Whatever else was in there tasted like dirty sweat socks. It was really bad. I have absolutely no doubt that this was done with the best of intentions, but was the overly salinized drink doing more harm than good? Yes, sweating as we all did, we definitely needed salt, but as they say … too much of a good thing. Today, science has proven the benefits of sports drinks such as Gatorade, but parent company PepsiCo isn't about to tell you what's in that either. At least Gatorade is palatable! But nowadays in the unrelenting desert heat, even at night and even during actual games, Arizona State University players eat oranges during games to ward off and/or treat cramps. No secret recipe there.

Practice proceeded as one might expect; stretches and warm-ups which invariably included Raider-jacks. We had a couple football dummies, those punching bag-looking things that they show people tackling in football movies. We didn't use them very much; mostly they were lain down and used as a boundary or barrier for some drill. When we did use them, we did not tackle them. The most actual use they ever had was when coaches would use them to help linemen practice their blocking technique. A coach would grab the strap handles and hold it in upright to evaluate how - and how well - a player blocked the dummy. Was he trying to block too upright? Was he off balance? Was he looking down or have his head up? If so, it was easier to see and fix, and less embarrassing than the inevitable result of man-to-man drills. Even more efficient was the seven-man sled. Sleds come in many sizes, but nearly all of them have a kind of vertical leaf-spring covered in padded canvas, representing an individual opponent. From a three-point stance, typically we were given three commands using a whistle blow: 1) hit the sled, 2) hit the sled, and then 3) hit and drive the sled until the coach blew the whistle a fourth time, which was often twenty yards or more down the practice field. We liked this most when it was or had been raining. The skids on the bottom of the sled glided across the slightest bit of water, even just damp grass. With dry ground, it was all work. The coaches who rode the sled to add weight to it knew this too, so we didn't use the sled as much when it wasn't dry out. Competition ensued however, because a seven-man sled is quite wide. So, at the third whistle, everyone tried to outpace each other. When that happened, the sled would cease going straight and start curving toward the side whose guys weren't keeping up. We took turns at the sled for a while, so that everyone got more than one crack at it.

Speaking of wet grass, a note about the practice fields and school grounds becomes relevant later. Below the grass virtually everywhere on the site was clay. Not loam, or even poor topsoil, just thick impermeable clay. When it rained, it sometimes took days for the ground to absorb the pools and puddles that had accumulated. So as a team, virtually everyone became accustomed to maintaining balance, blocking, tackling, and running routes in nearly any kind of sloppy and slippery mess, because every patch of ground where we practiced would quickly become a muddy challenge. Oftentimes we did this with our feet in an inch or two of standing water. Any earlier mentions of "swamp" are in reference to these conditions. Because we did this so often, we actually became so used to it that it became second nature; we didn't even think about it. It was akin to getting your sea legs or skateboarding, except that it was a combination of maintaining balance and traction. We all got muddier, but everything still got done while we learned to run, and block, and tackle in the slippery conditions.

The real torture device at practice was called the cage. The purpose of the cage was to train our technique at staying low and balanced out of a three-point stance to more effectively block an opponent. Someone had used 2-inch metal pipe to make an interconnected contraption with seven separate chutes or blocking lanes about the same width as the sled, one for each position on the line. The top wasn't more than about four feet high, if that, with pipes forming a crossbar at the entrance and exit of each chute, the latter's purpose is to make sure you stay low coming out of your stance in order to block your opponent low. So you had to bend down, almost crawl into one of the lanes, which you did according to your position on the offensive line. Opposing you outside the cage – and free to take any defensive stance he pleased - was another player who, upon the whistle, you had to block. You had to do this by first staying low enough so as not to hit the top of your helmet on the metal bar as you exited to make the block, and second by not stepping on the eight foot long one-by-twelve in the middle of each chute that extended from inside each lane outward. The purpose of the plank was to train you to keep your feet apart in order to maintain balance and a solid base that improved your ability to block. I would swear that someone had waxed every one of them however, because put the slightest toe or edge of your foot on the board and ... down you went. In or after a rain, it was even slicker. Generally, we just rotated through all the guys in our position to be either the blocker or the defender, but at some point, our coach had an interesting idea. Being both the split end coach (offensively) and the middle guard coach (defensively), he thought it would be fun for all of us svelte wide receivers to have to block the fireplug middle guards that he also coached. He chose Tyrone Davis, who played behind Allen Davis (no relation). Allen was better than really good, and his brother Tim had practically been a legend at linebacker for WWR, earning himself a scholarship to the University of Michigan. Ty was a quite capable middle guard himself and eager to vent some of his frustration by pummeling the receivers in the cages. He primed his forearm right at head-high as we exited the cage. So, those paint marks from the crossbar that I had on the *backside* of my helmet? Those were courtesy of one Tyrone Davis. Still, it was better than the one and only time the coach got Rick Kelly to do it. Rick was a large boy, one of our starting defensive tackles. After he slammed me back up and into the crossbar, I pretty much avoided having another go. Fortunately, he was not trying to hurt anyone.

Some guys liked hitting more than others and a few guys just absolutely lived for it. Another of our defensive tackles who was definitely in the 'live for it' category was a large muscular junior named Aaron Brown, whom everyone called "Chunky." However it happened that he got that nickname, he clearly had no objection to it, and anyone would tell you that the name fit. Coming back from a lunch break between practices one day with another player, we opened the large steel door leading downstairs. We had quickly learned that you had to be quiet coming back from lunch because the senior players would turn off all the lights and take a nap after lunch, and they did not appreciate being disturbed. So we were a little surprised after just a step or two down we heard a very loud "***UHHH!***" followed immediately by a huge "***BOOM!***" We weren't sure what was going on, and then heard another "***BOOM!***" and realized it was coming from further inside the concrete walkway. As we opened the second smaller steel door, we were surprised to find a light on and even more surprised to see the source of all the noise. There was Chunky at the corner of the walkway, down in a three-point stance, then with a loud grunt, slamming his bare forearm into the door to the physical plant equipment. *He* was the one who had put the dents in the industrial steel door – *with his forearm*. He paid us no attention whatsoever as we walked by him to the locker room and nobody dared to tell him to stop. Chunky later earned a scholarship and played linebacker at Ohio State, where there is no doubt he was solely responsible for giving several University of Michigan linemen a case of ringing in their ears that persists to this day.

We ate in the school's cafeteria, where a small staff prepared meals for the team and coaches. If nothing else, you went there during the break because it was cooler there than outside. The cafeteria's eating area had dozens of square Formica-topped tables with four chairs per table. The chairs were a fiberglass bucket that came up a little higher than mid-back, all in different dull pastel colors of the groovy '60s. The chairs had four round steel legs that angled front and back attached to the bottom. One day at lunch, Larry Mallory and another guy, Sam Stroud, started a yelling match near the end of the rows of cafeteria tables. No one could make out what they were arguing about because they were yelling very loudly over each other. In one quick motion, Larry grabbed the back of a chair with both hands, swung it over his head, and threw it downward at Sam. Just as quickly, Sam threw both hands up in a defensive move, just as two of the upside down chair's legs smacked perfectly into his two upraised hands. He seemed just as shocked as everyone else that he had caught the chair. He hadn't had time to think or turn his head more than a glance. The whole thing did not take two seconds and, unbelievably, no one was hurt or caught in the act, which was nothing but pure luck. Sam tossed the chair aside and they both started laughing at what had happened for a few seconds, then started back yelling at each other again as they walked away down the hall. When we returned to afternoon practice, they both seemed fine.

Each practice weaved into the memory of another, but at least we were playing real football. We were throwing, and catching, and blocking, and tackling, and all the time learning to function as a real team. Because some plays in the book required more coordinated timing, we sometimes ran those over and over. Our signature play, if there was one at the time, was the T Belly Counter Right. "T" referred to a standard T-formation, where the fullback was directly behind the quarterback, with the left and right halfbacks to his corresponding left and right. The four backs thus resemble a squatty, upside down "T" when it is illustrated in the playbook. Instead of a straight handoff, the Belly Counter

Right had both the fullback and the right halfback fake carrying the ball to the left, while the left halfback juked to the left before taking the ball into the heart of the right side of the unbalanced line, hence "Belly." The play worked well because A) not one, but two play actions to the left cued opposing defenses to pursue in that direction, B) the ball carrier was actually going the other way away from pursuit, and C) the ball carrier was running behind the strong side of our unbalanced line.

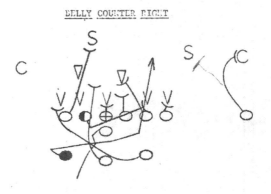

T Belly Counter Right, from our playbook.

The offense was led by quarterback and team co-captain Barry Simms. During games, the plays he called in the huddle came from Coach Novak via a headset connected to offensive coordinator Dick Lascola, who was up in the coaches' box. Each play was relayed to Barry by alternating split ends, typically Rick Houston, Don Henderson, or Burrell McGhee, and occasionally another senior. Jim King started at fullback, and John Hickman and Mike Spiva were halfbacks. Hickman functioned as an effective blocking back and had great hands when Barry's passes came his way. Spiva was an intuitive runner and was supported in his effectiveness because of Jim King's lead blocking. Henderson and McGhee were tall, lanky basketball players who would make excellent targets, except that on the few occasions that we did throw the ball, the pass likely went to tight end Ross Browner or to Hickman with his great hands and knack for getting open. The line was anchored by center Dennis Waltko, guards Bill Cleveland or Steve Ellis (left) and Dave Zimomra (right) who were spelled by Larry Rihel, with inside tackle Chris Mason, and outside tackle and co-captain Calvin Washington. Several others received a lot of playing time, including Marty Murray at fullback and linebacker and Chunky Brown at tackle.

The defense was a source of pride and tradition at WWR. With five down linemen and two linebackers, that put seven guys directly in opposition to any offensive formation. This meant that, although we had defensive schemes for man-to-man pass coverage, we nearly always had defensive backs playing zone coverage. That is, they each made sure they knew and were in their zone of responsibility and covering any potential receiver who entered that zone, versus following a specific assigned receiver to cover him.

Junior Ponce Henderson anchored the left defensive end position with Ross Browner on the right end. This seemed odd since nearly all offensive squads at all levels of football considered the right side of their offense - and therefore left side of the defense - their strong side. This was not because everyone had the same unbalanced line that we used, few did. It was because most quarterbacks were right-handed. However, as right defensive end, Ross defended the left side of the offense. It seemed unlikely because Ross Browner was – and I mean this in the absolute best of ways – a monster. He was a sculpted, muscular human being. The fact is, mention the 1972 team in any context to someone who had any connection to the team, and it is likely that the first name people will recall is Ross Browner. This probably has every bit as much to do with his later successes at the University of Notre Dame and the Cincinnati Bengals, but even in high school, people noticed and opponents knew Ross. The simple truth is that Ross Browner was the best football player on the field for every one of the twelve games that season. Although it's not as if Ponce was a downgrade at defensive end. He often hit people so hard in practice that we were concerned for the guy he tackled. Even the coaches would occasionally grimace at the sound of Ponce's hits.

Flanking middle guard Allen Davis, were two defensive tackles, through which rotated Rick Kelly, Cal Washington, or Chunky Brown. Dave Zimomra captained the defense at left linebacker, and either junior Marty Murray or Jim Browner, a sophomore and Ross's brother, on the right. The defensive backfield featured cornerbacks Rick Peterson and John Hickman, with Greg Patterson and Terry Roberts at safety. If you were to refer to the home game programs each week, you may notice that a few names are different. The program names apparently were provided before the first game, presumably as expected starters, but never changed for subsequent home game programs. So, for whatever reason, they were not necessarily correct.

We did not dedicate a lot of time to special teams. There were only basic special team plays in the playbook. We got chalkboard lectures - real vintage Vince Lombardi stuff - of who did what. If you were on punt or kickoff coverage, it was basically, "Run as hard as you can and get the guy with the ball." For punt and kickoff returns, we had a Return Left or a Return Right, which meant the kick returner followed the blockers and tried to avoid opponents in the general direction specified. We would do only a couple run-throughs each Friday practice since most of our games were on Saturday, to make sure we knew how to do it in theory and that was about it.

Bill Williams, a junior tackle had already proven himself as a placekicker for field goals and extra points. Nearly everyone in high school at the time still kicked the ball straight-on. When we eventually played a team from Youngstown whose kicker did it soccer style, everyone watched his warm-ups like it was an opening circus act. Bill wore a special squared-toe shoe on his right foot for kicking, as almost all straight ahead kickers did. As a back-up placekicker, sophomore Bill Huston also wore a kicking shoe on which he wrapped a shoelace around the cleat at the big toe and tied it off around his calf, to further raise up the blunt end of the shoe. This allowed him to get a lot more air under his kicks.

He once kicked an extra point so far and so high it went through the uprights on the south end of Mollenkopf Stadium and over the band shell that was beyond the track that wound outside the field, and then over the chain link fence behind that. The band shell was a unique set of bleachers expressly for the band which was adorned with a kind of pointy "W" (for Warren) trimming the front, and which was at least 30 feet high. His kick may have been aided by the fact that high school placekickers legally used a two-inch-high block of rubber as a placekicking tee.

Sophomores who were specifically on the varsity team were Jim Browner, Brian DeCree, and Ed Manusakis. Jim usually started at right linebacker. This ruffled a couple other players' feathers, one in particular, but there wasn't any doubt about who should be playing linebacker. He also kicked the ball off, and thus was beneficial as a formidable tackler when he did. Defensive end Brian DeCree was the younger brother of Van DeCree, who had graduated from Reserve in 1971 and was then starting at the same position for Ohio State. Ed Manusakis was the team punter from day one. Just a year earlier, in the freshman game against Harding that had ended in a 0-0 tie, Ed made a legendary 80 yard punt from his own end zone that very likely helped prevent a loss.

Somehow, someway a fascinating detail of this season has lost every reference to it. A week or two before our first game, we loaded up a couple busses and set off to Massillon to have a scrimmage against their players at their facilities. The coaches announced we were going more or less as a surprise, and did so in Pavlovian anticipation. They *really* relished this opportunity. Somehow our school officials had convinced the state's perennial power that if they wouldn't schedule us to play them in a real game, then why not a scrimmage ... and they had agreed. It was a huge surprise; the coaches were almost giddy at the unprecedented opportunity. It did not appear that it was planned very far in advance, because we basically didn't know anything about it until we were told we were going. After the long bus ride, we unloaded the busses and all of our gear and got dressed, but even before we had started warmups, we heard thunder. The weather quickly turned nasty, and the scrimmage was called off because of the storm. Everyone on both teams was disappointed. Our coaches thought they had a real chance to gauge the performance of the team against a more-or-less known quality team, and as players, we wanted to have a crack at the legend. All of that seemed gone literally in a matter of minutes. Ironically, thanks to the new playoff system, we almost had a real game with Massillon; *the* real game.

That bit of unfortunateness did not matter neither here nor there in terms of history, which may be the reason it has been lost over the years. A more serious matter was an injury to a player in practice that happened at some point near the start of the season. It's a bit of a haunting memory, because I saw them doing the drills mere moments before it happened. In expectation of our first game, the sophomore team was drilling separately from the varsity. We finished early that day and were let go, as the varsity continued practicing on the other fields. As I walked home, I passed right by where the varsity linemen were practicing game-simulated blocking on each other; that is, down in their stance and – quite literally – head butting each other at the whistle. It was just a one-on-one test of ability and manhood. The technique that was taught to us repeatedly was always to use the crown of your forehead to block or tackle, but we were told the next day that Matt Miller, a junior lineman, had dropped his head (looked down) just before his opponent made contact. Because his head and eyes were down, he was hit on the very top of his helmet. Whether that explanation was accurate or true or not, that was what we were told. The injury appeared to have had some lasting effect on his motor skills and so his playing days were over. The coaches hounded us even more on proper technique from that day forward, screaming "Head up!" more often, over and over.

The varsity began the season as we always did, with a home game against Cleveland Collinwood. It was rumored that some sort of deal with ticket proceeds was made which assured us of a first game, home game and Collinwood of better proceeds each season. They were the only team we did not play home-and-away in alternating years. Next up was Austintown Fitch High School, for whom we were their big rival. Third was Barberton, our first North East Ohio Conference rival, and fourth we played at home against Jamestown, New York. We held all four teams scoreless, to a point total of 84-0 for those four games. During the second week of the season, the sophomores played what we were told afterward would be our only game that year, beating Akron Hoban on our home practice field. I remember the game mostly for the play in which I tackled one of their running backs, who then promptly jumped right back up and stepped on my hand with his cleat before I could get up because another player had piled in behind me as we all went down along the sideline. We had an eight game schedule printed, with an additional open date, but the reason given for cancelling the rest of our season was that we did not have enough players. However, they had cancelled the season right after a game in which we obviously had enough players, and which we had won. As it turned out, we didn't mind. We all started dressing for every varsity game shortly after that.

We still played other games because we were included in the Junior Varsity games which were a short schedule, intended to evaluate the non-starters and keep them in playing, rather than practicing, condition. A week and a half after the Hoban game, we travelled to Canton McKinley for a JV game. It turned into a nightmare, and I couldn't even tell you how the game went. The school bus turned into the parking lot at Fawcett Stadium, right next to the Pro Football Hall of Fame. We thought, 'All right, this could be fun!' We were ushered into a locker room to change, but could not believe what we saw. Without exaggeration, it was a dump. Filthy, small lockers, broken and nonfunctional, it was the single worst locker room I have ever seen by a wide margin. I remember thinking right then and there that there was no way pro football players used this during the Hall of Fame game, or even that visiting high school coaches found it acceptable. The closest comparison I could possibly make is to the men's room at the old Cleveland Municipal Stadium. Yes, it was that bad. Disappointment number two: We were not using the stadium field. We would play in a gravel-filled space next to the stadium that was obviously used for parking. It was literally a field of rocks and gravel everywhere, with sprigs of grass here and there. We were all thinking, "We have to tackle guys in this?"

Then – and I'm not blaming him, just relating how it happened - during blocking drills that we did in warm-ups, Joe DiGiovanni didn't wait for the "Set" and just went, but I was still not quite primed for the contact. Unprepared, my hand was still right in front of me and he blocked it with his helmet into my shoulder pads. Although I didn't know it at the time, I had broken a chip off the bone at the base of my thumb. What I did know was that the pain was excruciating. I went directly to the trainer who accompanied us to games – presumably specifically for such a situation - but he merely glanced at it and said, "You're fine" and walked away. I told him I wasn't but he kept walking away to do nothing but get a good vantage point to watch the start of the game. I did not know that I had broken something, but I knew for certain that I was not fine. Because apparently it was worth its weight in gold, I had to demand and practically threaten the equipment manager to give me athletic tape. I wrapped my thumb myself, and then just stayed out of the way.

I went to my personal doctor who took an X-ray in which I could clearly see for myself a chip floating by itself at the base of the thumb. It did not help that the break was on my writing hand and the following week, standardized testing was scheduled for everyone in my grade. I could barely hold a pencil, much less write. To be clear, in 1972, standardized testing meant using a #2 pencil to fill in your answers to what seemed like endless questions, mostly multiple-choice. I taped my thumb in combination with a pad over it for the rest of the season.

Next up for the varsity was the rivalry game against Harding. As if we needed another reminder, after the first practice that week, Ross Browner and inside tackle Chris Mason (and probably other seniors) went around the locker room distributing armbands to each member of the team. They were red with "15-8" in black.

We wore them in school each day that week. Both sides were disappointed that Harding did not come into the game undefeated - having already lost to Steubenville - but that did not diminish our desire to avenge the prior year's loss. After winning the matchup in the prior year for the first time, Harding's new mantra was, "Never Again." In reality, "Never Again" came to mean roughly once every three years, so that slogan quickly disappeared. But during Harding week practice, a small plane flew over the practice fields at what is probably an illegally low altitude and spewed hundreds of flyers all over, with the wind taking them in all directions. The flyers were hand written mimeographed Tokyo Rose kind of nonsense: "Never Again!" "You can't win." "Panther Pride!", and other such senseless and meaningless propaganda. It was bad enough once, but as I recall they did it again the next year too.

With the city of Warren a nexus of divided loyalties, tickets for this game were once again sold out. We alternated each year with Harding as to which team was the 'home' team, but in all practical matters, the only differences were which side of the field the teams were on, and which team's band got to use the band shell, instead of the rickety temporary stands placed on the track behind the visitor's side. The other nulling aspect of home/visitor distinction was that supporters of both schools could purchase their season tickets on either side of the stadium. So, even if it was a Harding home game, there were many season ticket holders on the visitor side because they could get better seats (i.e. closer to midfield). It was likewise for many WWR fans who found themselves surrounded by "visitors" from just the other side of town. In fact, many of the WWR fans on that side probably had a longer drive home than most of the "visiting" Panther fans. In one of the Harding seats behind us for the game was our close family friends' relative, visiting from Australia. Bob was a tall, well-nourished, and highly stereotypical Aussie who had played rugby in his not too distant past. He came to the game with an in-law of the family - a Harding grad - whose season tickets were on the visiting side.

Even though Mollenkopf Stadium was directly adjacent to the high school at that time, for every game we played there – all of them – we never used the school's facilities. We were always sent to a dank corner on the north side underneath the visitor's side seats. We arrived each time half-dressed, simply put on the shoulder pads and helmets that we had carried with us on the bus, having donned the rest of our uniforms and had our ankles taped, etc. in our own locker room across town. Even as the home team for our other games, we went to that same small corner with just a few wooden benches in it. Essentially we were visitors in our own stadium. Our visiting teams (except Harding) went to what I certainly hope was a more reasonably sized and complete locker room, further down on the same side. Harding's team always went out the north end zone and directly into the high school to their regular locker room.

As a team, we pretty much knew that the game would not be a pushover shutout such as we had enjoyed a couple times in the first four games of the season. For the sellout crowd, it did not disappoint. Sustained drives on both sides ended the first half with Harding leading 14-13. Both sides used more pass plays than might have been expected, but it was defense, and in particular, special teams play that won the game. When one of our drives was stopped, Ed Manusakis came in to punt on fourth down. The play was the first of two in the game that almost spelled disaster. As if in slow motion, the long snap to Ed looked as though it was clearly going to sail well over his head. Ed leaped straight up, reaching every bit as high as he possibly could and just barely touched the ball enough with the tip of his fingers. As he fell back down to the ground, the ball dropped down into his hands and as he tucked it away, started running to his left. The crowd noise for that game was equal to the occasion, so most of our team did not realize that the ball had not been punted. As a result, many of them were running down to cover what they thought was a kicked ball, but Ed was running as fast as I've ever seen him run. He was evading Harding tacklers who had seen the miscue, on his way to getting a first down and a few yards extra. Ed's reaction and quick thinking was the first instance in which arguably the game had been saved. He didn't even glance to see if he might try to punt; he didn't want a blocked kick and knew he had to get the first down himself.

In the second half, our special teams came up big again, this time on defense when Allen Davis blocked a Harding punt. This essentially set up the winning drive that included two pass plays, when halfback Mike Spiva ran the ball in for a touchdown. The touchdown made the score 19-14, so we pretty much had to go for a two point play and were successful, making it 21-14. With less than a minute to go, that's how the game ended, but that almost didn't happen. Earlier, Harding had driven all the way down the field with goal to go, and threw a pass to a receiver coming across into the middle of the end zone. The pass was not high, but the receiver still jumped up to catch it against his body underhand in the crook of his elbow. We used to rag on each other mercilessly any time someone did this in practice, because we called it 'styling' – trying to show style, but mostly because it was poor technique. Actually, we always said it as *stylin'*. It was too easy to misjudge the ball and have it slip right past your elbow, which did in fact happen a lot in practice, and which garnered a repeat lecture about catching the ball with your hands. You should catch a football with your hands - period. First of all, the pass was not thrown very high. He neither had to overreach for it, nor should he have had to leave the ground to catch it. He could – and should – have easily caught the ball by raising his hands just above shoulder level. Jumping up and *stylin'* as he did, the very instant the ball thumped into his elbow, he and the ball were hit head-on by one of the safeties, I believe Greg Patterson, whose feet were firmly on the ground and the ball popped out before the receiver's feet touched the ground. Officials immediately ruled the pass incomplete. I learned innumerable insights from him, but this is the solitary time to my knowledge that Coach Novak had been mistaken. When we reviewed game film on Monday, he insisted that we had caught a lucky break because, he said, "That was a touchdown." Intrigued, I went to watch him review the game film with the Booster Club and a couple days later at the Quarterback Club, and he said almost word for word the same thing. He said, because it was over the plane of the end zone, that the moment the ball was caught, the play was over. But under OHSAA rules, for a pass to be complete in high school – to be "caught" - a player must have control of the ball and at least one foot in bounds. It does not matter whether the ball is over the plane of the end zone or not, it still must first be a completed pass. For it to have been a completed touchdown pass, it must first be a completed pass. It was not a catch, and therefore not a touchdown, because he did not touch the ground before the ball came loose, which was clear even in the grainy black-and-white game film of the day. In fact because the receiver had jumped in the first place, Greg's slightly upward hit probably helped to momentarily assist in preventing the receiver's feet from touching the ground, and with that, Harding's momentum pretty much ended. Harding scored no points on that drive, or at any other time in the second half.

When the clock ran out, it was pandemonium. Students flooded onto the field, and seemingly instantly everyone at the same time realized what the victory meant. We had just defeated the defending AP state champs: WE were number one! There were so many people on the field you could barely move, and every one of them had their index finger pointed in the air. People were slapping us on the back or on the helmet, or trying to jump on our backs. It was nearly impossible to move and we had to force our way through the crowd to get to the locker room. As I approached the locker room door, a few remaining members of our band were still in the temporary visiting band bleacher next to it and I thought I heard someone yelling my name. I looked up and saw a friend from the band bent over the flimsy rail screaming to me from the top row and at the top of his lungs, "We're Number One!" over and over again. I could barely hear him from the chants of the rest of the crowd, but just pointed my finger back at him. I walked through the door and wondered where everyone was. The only other person in the room was Coach Novak, who had gone as far as he could go into the farthest corner and was sitting on a bench looking wide-eyed down at the floor with a huge grin on his face. After a moment or two he glanced up, acknowledging that someone else was there, then just put his head back down, almost as if in disbelief. More likely, it was relief and pure satisfaction.

When we got back to our basement locker room at WWR, everyone was hooting and hollering in no hurry to shower and change, when as if by magic, Barry Simms appeared shaking a can of spray paint in his hand. Almost instantly the volume went up as everyone knew what he was going to do. Amid cheers and slaps on the back, he and Co-Captain Cal Washington walked over to the center of the room and sprayed black paint over the red "15-8" on the floor. Every single bit of physical and mental effort for the last year had been put almost singularly into this moment, and we as a team were finally free of the burden. Even the coaches joined in the cheers.

A day or two later I saw Bob again, whose only comment on anything about the game was, "The better team lost." I just retorted to him that the same thing happened last year ... when they had won. I shrugged it off as his being unfamiliar with the American game, and more likely undue influence from the Harding ticket holder with whom he had gone to the game. When we won the playoff championship weeks after he had returned home, I sent him a shirt so he'd be sure to know which team was better.

About this time, we started getting occasional volunteer help at practice. Vern Wireman was a 1966 (and therefore pre-rivalry) Harding graduate who had gone on to be a three-year starting quarterback at Bowling Green State University. In doing so, he lit up both the school and the conference passing records. He would help out when he could we were told, since he was still playing in a semi-pro industrial league somewhere. Help he did. He was mainly beneficial for quarterbacking the scout team pass plays against our secondary. Actually, beneficial isn't the right term; Breath of fresh air starts in the right direction. Unlike our coaches, who would rather be coaching anyway, Vern could throw the ball ... accurately and in nice tight spirals. No offense to our coaches, but I would occasionally go after and catch balls that were lobbed in practice for which I'm not entirely sure I was the intended receiver. The scout sessions against our defensive secondary suddenly became livelier and more realistic. Instead of chasing after an errant thrown ball, we could run sharp patterns, and the ball would be there. He once threw a ball behind me because I made a cut early in order to get clear of our cornerback and I still caught it because we quickly got used to his rhythm and timing, and I knew exactly where the ball would be. The opponents' pass plays were drawn out on white poster board sheets that came from our assistant coaches who had scouted opponents and from the game film each high school team was required to provide the other in advance. There is no doubt that Wireman helped our starting secondary prepare better, and he made practice more fun in the process. Unfortunately, he was only available to be there occasionally.

The reminder of the regular season featured four North East Ohio Conference opponents, including Akron St. Vincent-St. Mary. St. Vincent was a little shrewd with their scheduling. Despite being a Class AA (medium sized) high school, they scheduled nearly all of their games with Class AAA opponents, partly facilitated by being in a conference with nothing but Class AAA teams. Although we beat them definitively during the season, they ultimately became the first Class AA playoff champions. If the name Akron St. Vincent sounds familiar: Thirty or so years later their football team briefly had a tall, athletic receiver named LeBron James. I understand the kid never went to college. I hope he made out okay.

Two weeks after the Harding game, and after the varsity had beaten St. Vincent, the coaches told the sophomores we would have another game after all. The freshman team was playing the Harding freshman team on Thursday at Mollenkopf, and they had decided to let us play their sophomores on the same night as was originally scheduled, since the stadium, the officials ... everything was already in place. The rookies would play and then we would play, and the fans would get two more rivalry games for the price of one. Not the least of the problems with this news was that we sophomores hadn't practiced together as a unit in more than a month, and had undoubtedly lost another person or two in the interim. During most of that time, some of us were running scout team offense against our starting defense, and others of us on a different part of the field were doing just the opposite for our offense week after week. We had been practicing with the varsity team, and since our schedule was cancelled, our backfield for instance, wasn't going to take away any of the reps from the first and second teamers. The freshman had always been practicing together. Rules at the time prohibited freshmen from playing varsity football; perhaps they still do. Probably there is an age rule, perhaps as well as having something to do with that fact that in many Ohio school districts, 9th graders were in middle school, whereas in many others, such as Warren's, they were in high school. In any case, not only were they more prepared as a unit, they perennially had Dave Campbell coaching them, who made them even more prepared to beat Harding specifically. Which they did.

We arrived for the game nonetheless, had to wait for the game to end, then had to wait as each member of the freshman team walked over and threw their game-used jersey into a pile that we then had to rummage through for our number. After that, we could finally warm-up a bit, which was also rushed because everyone else was ready and eager to get the second game going. The result, somewhat obviously, was that we did not impress. It didn't help that the newly distributed jerseys we were wearing were a perforated synthetic. They looked fine, but soon after the game started, our running backs almost immediately complained. The fabric was some kind of '70s rubbery synthetic and was so sticky that our backs could not break free from tackles if an opponent only got a hand on their jersey. It was similar to using a silicone jar lid opener to get an effective grip. It had that much of a tacky effect. The real problem though was Harding's team had been practicing together as a unit for months and we had not. We soldiered through, but came up short.

The varsity team continued to roll against NEOC opponents Akron Hoban, then Cuyahoga Falls. Against Falls, we were leading 14-0 with barely any time left in the game, when we once again took over the ball on offense. Coach Novak was simply trying to run out the clock, calling repeated running plays and then a screen pass to the left which he envisioned as simply taking more time to develop and thereby helping to run the clock down. When he relayed the play via one of our split ends, he also reminded him to make sure we stayed in bounds. As soon as the play started to develop, Coach went from thoughtful and satisfied to panic-stricken. When John Hickman caught the ball in the flat, there were no defenders ahead of him. This was probably because they were both expecting another running play and therefore bunched at the line of scrimmage, as well as fatigued and distraught at being shut out. Coach Novak started screaming, "NO! NO!" at the top of his lungs the entire time as Hickman caught the ball and scooted easily down the field for another score as the clock ran out. Even before the whistle, he was running toward the referee waving his hands back and forth, motioning that we were declining the point-after attempt. The ref at first seemed perplexed, but as soon as he understood what Coach wanted, he signaled that the game was over. But Coach Novak never stopped running. After acknowledgment from the official, he ran immediately to the opposite sideline to apologize profusely to the Falls coach over the play call, explaining that he had only wanted to run out the clock. Coach Novak was visibly embarrassed that, however accidentally, we had run up the score on a defeated opponent.

During the final week of the varsity season while preparing for conference rival Lorain Southview, several of the players started using the term Senior Hit and pointing at one or another player. One might say that Senior Hit was a rite of passage for the football team. Each senior, in a one-at-a-time ritual display, picked one underclassman to stand about five yards away and get tackled. A more correct description was that the person chosen was not so much tackled as laid out by the senior, who ran the short, but highly effective distance straight at him. It quickly became apparent that many of the seniors had at some point been the victim of the ritual, and each was eager to pass the tradition along to someone else. The senior player started from a three-point stance while the victim (not sure there's a better word for it) stood upright, knees bent in a relaxed but braced stance and for lack of another term, took it. One by one, coaches would call each senior by name, who would then announce the name of the person they had chosen. Often players had a hint as to who was picking whom, but part of the "fun" was that no one knew for sure that they were the target until their name was called. The ritual continued until all seniors had their hit. Some guys took a particularly vicious hit and jumped right up jaw-boning back "it was nothing," or "is that all you got," or similar retorts. Most just got up without saying anything, happy it was over. But for some underclassmen it wasn't over, because some were called more than once. No one was badly hurt that day, but it wasn't because of a lack of enthusiasm.

At the very last practice before the final game, a more honorable ritual occurred. We ran basic plays as each senior was called by name one or two at a time after each play and, then was replaced by an underclassman and excused from practice. Each senior walked past a line the coaches had formed and shook each hand as he went. It was a ceremonial changing of the guard. The coaches were thanking and recognizing each and every senior player for their efforts. For the rest of us, practice continued a while after all of the seniors were excused.

Talk about the playoffs was occurring everywhere, and as with anything new, nobody really understood whether WWR had a chance to be selected or not. All the team could do was to try to win what could be the last game of the year. The following evening, a 28-0 victory over Lorain Southview meant that our record was a perfect 10-0. In the ten games of the regular season, we had outscored our opponents 249-53. In just the year before, rival Harding had their first undefeated and untied season after having played 78 seasons of high school football. WWR had done it in just their seventh year, and had come within a single game in four of the other six seasons. How did this happen? What set the tone and energized not just one, but both schools from a relatively small and relatively unknown city to this level of success? No question: it was the result of a raging cross-town rivalry that drove everyone to be a better football player.

In the month of November in 1972, WWR completed its first undefeated football schedule, eighteen year-olds would vote in a presidential election for the first time ever, and the Ohio High School Athletic Association would hold its very first championship playoff games. Before the month was over, WWR would achieve another first.

6

CHAMPIONS

From the start in 1972, either modifications were made by the OHSAA to Jack Harbin's system or what was explained to the public was incorrect. Multiple sources indicate that high school teams earned first level points for beating an opponent and second level points for the opponents' beaten opponents. Third level points were then extended another level from that, to be used only to break a tie of the total of first and second level points. As you can see from OHSAA's records and as should be expected, the third level points increase almost exponentially, but were unmistakably used to determine the regional winners. It actually made a difference in Region 2. It was third level points – without any tie to break – that allowed Toledo Scott into the playoffs. Even more curious is that the point totals of all three levels were used *only* in the first two years of the system. In 1974 and every year thereafter, the playoff entrant in each region has been based on the total of just first and second level points.

WEEK 10	CLASS AAA	REGION 1				
RANK	HIGH SCHOOL NAME		LEVEL 1	LEVEL 2	LEVEL 3	TOTAL
1	WARREN WESTERN RESERVE		29	158	671	858
2	EASTLAKE NORTH		27	136	578	741
3	PARMA SENIOR		27	132	541	700
4	CLEVELAND ST. IGNATIUS		26	133	517	676
5	LAKEWOOD ST EDWARD		23	110	539	672

WEEK 10	CLASS AAA	REGION 2				
RANK	HIGH SCHOOL NAME		LEVEL 1	LEVEL 2	LEVEL 3	TOTAL
1	TOLEDO SCOTT		27	112	472	611
2	TOLEDO CENTRAL CATHOLIC		27	127	406	560
3	FREMONT ROSS		27	117	391	535
4	SANDUSKY		24	104	374	502
5	COLUMBUS EASTMOOR		22	99	368	489

WEEK 10	CLASS AAA		REGION 3				
RANK	HIGH SCHOOL NAME			LEVEL 1	LEVEL 2	LEVEL 3	TOTAL
1	MASSILLON WASHINGTON			30	185	866	1081
2	CUYAHOGA FALLS WALSH JESUIT			27	148	551	726
3	AKRON GARFIELD			26	128	504	658
4	CANTON MCKINLEY			24	128	479	631
5	ZANESVILLE			24	112	473	609

WEEK 10	CLASS AAA		REGION 4				
RANK	HIGH SCHOOL NAME			LEVEL 1	LEVEL 2	LEVEL 3	TOTAL
1	CINCINNATI PRINCETON			30	160	532	722
2	TROY			27	133	543	703
3	KETTERING FAIRMONT EAST			27	121	494	642
4	CINCINNATI ELDER			29	138	439	606
5	CINCINNATI MOELLER			24	107	426	557

Top five from each region, reproduced from the final OHSAA 1972 computer rankings, available on their site. (www.ohsaa.org)

Based on first and second level points, the Region 2 entry to the first state playoff should have been Toledo Central Catholic with 154 pts, to Scott's 139. In fact Toledo Scott should have finished third, because third-listed Fremont Ross had 144 points. In 1973, the same thing happened, but in Region 3. Ironically, because the 1973 rankings also used the total of first, second, and third level points, WWR missed - for the third time in little over 15 months - yet another opportunity to play Massillon. In 1974, the OHSAA's official rankings record ceased reporting the third level points.

The digitized printouts from OHSAA's website, are what remain as the official historical record of the event, and Jack Harbin's name is nowhere to be found – neither on these printouts after 1984, nor today anywhere on the OHSAA website. On the back of the very first, very plain championship playoff game programs sold by the OHSAA in 1972, an explanation of the ranking system is found. It is titled, "The Harbin Football Rating System as used by the Ohio High School Athletic Association."

* * * * *

Word spread quickly: Warren Western Reserve was in the playoffs. We had at least one more game to play, and the OHSAA had arranged the initial set of playoff games to take place in Ohio State University's football stadium. Because of its shape, it was and still is affectionately referred to as "the Horseshoe." OHSAA rules necessitated some adjustments and disappointing choices. Ohio Stadium featured an artificial grass surface that we generically referred to as AstroTurf at the time. This was something with which we had no experience.

As noted earlier, every team was required to use a standard football, which was not really an inconvenience to any of us. The thing that hurt for many players was that the state had restricted the number of players each team could bring to each playoff game to 44. Coach Novak was the one who ultimately had to make the decisions about who was in and who wasn't.

Coach Novak may have had the responsibility, but he also did not appreciate the restriction and openly said so. He told the team as much, and he told the Boosters and Quarterback Club that he knew how hard every member of the team had worked to get us to this point and was disappointed that everyone could not be included. With the unusual absorption of the sophomore team that season however, the contingent would have been unusually large by any standard. Even at the time, we all understood that he had many more and bigger things to occupy his attention for the next week, so 44 players it would be. Arrangements were being made to stay overnight so that the team would be fresh to play in the most important game that many might ever be in. But a matter of immediate urgency for the team was to practice at least once on artificial turf ... somewhere. None of the players and few of the coaches had ever played on an artificial grass field. This also meant that new shoes were an urgent need for the 44 players going, because most football shoes were made for grass fields and that was all we had at the start of the week. The broad and rigid knobs that protruded from the bottom of football cleats were designed to dig into grass and dirt surfaces. On relatively uniform and flat artificial surfaces, they did not work very well, and potentially could be damaging to the grass carpet. Shoes with many more uniformly pliable rubbery nubs were needed for traction on artificial grass. Somehow, by mid-week, the turf-style shoes were passed out, all of them new in the box.

At the time, sports fans were just getting used to seeing artificial turf on their television sets in some college and in many multi-use professional stadiums. Artificial surfaces were not nearly as prevalent in the early 70s, certainly for high schools. When the Astrodome, Houston's so-called "eighth wonder of the world" opened in 1965, the immense playing field inside was replaced with AstroTurf (literally the brand name Monsanto had given it) when the natural grass first installed there quickly died. But it was still relatively new and something to which purists tended to object, and so it was slow to gain the ubiquitous acceptance it has today.

Modern artificial surfaces are wonderful in comparison to the choices that were available in the early 1970s. At the time, seams between sections typically didn't meet properly, which could and would cause injuries. Some brands of turf were manufactured with better padding underneath, and others had none at all. The competing brand Poly-Turf at the (original) Orange Bowl was alleged to have melted in spots at times from Miami's intense heat. Even Mollenkopf Stadium now has artificial grass, but in 1972, the problem was that in Northeast Ohio there were hardly any fields with an artificial surface.

Therefore said school officials, it wasn't easy to find a facility that that was both close enough and willing to let the team practice there – even just once. The answer came as a surprise. The Cleveland Browns used the artificial turf field at Baldwin Wallace College in Berea for their regular practices. Team officials were willing to let WWR use the field after they were done with it themselves one afternoon later in the week. The Browns had a practice facility adjacent to the field which was equally utilitarian for the team, since they played on artificial surfaces regularly against division opponents Pittsburgh and Cincinnati, as well as others throughout the league. Coach Novak was almost giddy with the news, joking that he was hoping to talk them into having a short scrimmage with us. It also turned out to be the perfect solution. The facility was relatively close, an hour's bus ride, secure from any prying eyes, well maintained, and the turf itself was relatively new. This meant that the field itself was in excellent condition, despite regular, almost daily use by real professionals.

That week, practice went more or less normally for a couple days. There were no ceremonial displays and very little horseplay; everything was businesslike with solemn undertones, despite a few people trying to keep the mood light. A difference was the contrast from the mid-summer two-a-days. By mid-November, it was regularly both windy and cold. Snow flurries hinting at the coming of winter occasionally fell. To compensate, many players started taping up the earholes in their helmets and wearing two pairs of socks, with any plastic bag you could find between the two layers. The plastic bag kept the inside sock dry*(-ish)*, which helped considerably with preventing your feet from getting cold in the persistently wet conditions of the practice fields. On either Wednesday or Thursday, our coaches and the 44 man playoff roster boarded two city school busses for their one-time afternoon practice on Baldwin Wallace's artificial turf field. On Friday morning, November 17, all classes were temporarily suspended for a massive pep rally and sendoff for the team. The school board had decided to charter two plush commercial tour busses for the team's trip to Columbus. They had decided that this was an event of sufficient significance to have the team "go first class." A sizable portion of the band played the fight song over and over, as hundreds of students thronged to the tiny south parking area and surrounded the busses, while Coach Novak tried to thank everyone for their support.

The team would stay overnight in Columbus, and would play in the second of two Class AAA playoff games on Saturday against Toledo's Scott High School. The first game at around 11:00am would pit Massillon against Cincinnati's Princeton High. Massillon had won the AP poll at the end of the regular season, and had –

according to Harbin's algorithm – the most points of any class AAA team in any of the four regions. WWR would play Toledo Scott after the 11:00am game ended, tentatively scheduled for 2:00pm.

In retrospect, because they could not have known it at the time, this was the day that things started going off the rails for the Massillon Washington Tigers; so far off that they effectively have never truly recovered. Earlier that week, Massillon won the AP state championship poll for the 13th, *and last*, time in the 26 years of the poll's existence to that point. Fully *half* of the AP mythical championships went to the Tigers. In the fifty years since that 1972 poll, they would not win another. The following year in 1973, the poll rankings show that their second place 661.8 points meant that they missed a second straight trip to the playoffs by only 5.5 points. Perhaps they were ones who got the rule changed, because they missed the playoffs as a result of the OHSAA using the total of first, second, and third level points. If the calculations had been made the way they were initially intended, and the way it would be used *every* year thereafter – based on first and second level points only and using third level points in the event of a tie - they would have won their region by 12 points (or about 8 percent).

The game that day did not go their way either. Cincinnati Princeton was a powerhouse with a strong running back named Mike Gayles, and the whole team looked extremely comfortable on artificial turf, but Massillon was used to the spotlight and equal to the task. Both teams had two touchdowns with the game ultimately decided by a Princeton field goal, making the final score 17-14. Massillon's loss in the first Class AAA playoff would also ostensibly mean that WWR had, in a matter of mere weeks, missed a second chance to play the Tigers. Now just a footnote to the rivalry that never was: the following year in 1973 the teams missed a third opportunity to play when Massillon was locked out of the playoffs by 5.5 points (just 8/10ths of 1 percent).

Cleveland rocks and numbers don't lie. The 8/10ths of 1 percent difference is concrete empirical evidence that Harbin's strength of schedule algorithm works and makes a strong case that using all three level points in the first two years was both the correct thing and that it should have been *the right thing* to do going forward. Arguably, most anyone concerned should gladly trade a missed opportunity to play a given team for getting the right participants into the system correctly, particularly when teams within a given region end the season with exactly the same win-loss record. But the reality in any case is that Massillon had to win out ... and they didn't.

After their game ended, instead of staying to watch the second playoff game between WWR and Toledo Scott, many of the Massillon fans simply and solemnly left. But on his way out, one lone Massillon fan, an early middle-aged gentleman in a black Massillon jacket, slowly walked up the steps between sections in the stadium and across a few of the aisles, saying only the same three words to every WWR-clad fan that he noticed, "Bring it back!" Translation: Bring the trophy back to Northeast Ohio. I wish I knew who that man was to give him the credit, because not only was it a true and rare act of sportsmanship, it was also more than a hint that the entire Massillon fan base had been champing at the bit[13] for a matchup with WWR as badly as we had been for them. It never happened.

Toledo Scott had a very good team and proved as much by outpacing WWR to a 15-0 lead in just the first quarter. By sheer happenstance in the days leading up to the game, Coach Novak had related to numerous interviewers that, ideally, he would like to be up 15-0, because it required two touchdowns and two 2-point conversions to overcome the deficit. As it happened however, in Columbus on that November afternoon, the tables were turned on his druthers. But WWR's defensive and offensive coordinators were among the best, which may be one man's opinion, but the results bear this out. Coaches Bud Myers and Dick Lascola quickly made adjustments in-game and at halftime, resulting in the

---

[13] Yes, champing is in fact the correct term and yes, pun intended.

second quarter and the second half looking like an entirely different game from the team's play in the first quarter. First the defense rose up and then the offense found its rhythm. Both the ideal playing conditions and the situation dictated using the passing game more, which successfully capped a sustained drive before the half with tight end Ross Browner catching the touchdown. But Toledo's earlier steady offensive progress ground to a halt and the 15 points scored in the first quarter were all they would manage for the rest of the game. In the third quarter, the two teams played to a draw.

The turning point of the game came in the fourth quarter with the score still 15-8 in favor of Toledo. All by itself, that particular score was foreboding to the Raiders and probably helped turn the team up to the proverbial eleven. The Bulldogs were gaining momentum driving toward the north end zone when they attempted a screen pass to their offense's left side of the field. Raging through feigned blocks that were meant to set up Toledo's screen to that side were Chunky Brown and Ross Browner. At possibly the very last instance to realize what was happening and still prevent it, Ross was coming off the end and glimpsed the back running past in the opposite direction toward the flat. Realizing he was extremely close but making no attempt to block him, Ross suddenly understood what was happening and reached out with his arm. Nearly swiping the back with his hand in the process, he changed direction to pursue him. At the same moment, Toledo's quarterback had started to raise the ball to throw the screen, but seeing Ross' pursuit made him hesitate to throw and he tucked the ball away ... to his own peril. At defensive tackle, Chunky was further inside on a full-out bull rush and neither saw the back, nor the screen forming. He simply made a bee-line to the quarterback as he started to tuck the ball away and pummeled him into the turf. The play resulted in a sack, the drive stalled, and with it, Toledo's spirit had visibly been broken. From that moment forward, WWR was firmly in control of the game. Two sustained drives later made the final score 23-15. WWR had won and would play Cincinnati Princeton for the very first Class AAA playoff championship in Ohio's history.

The championship game would be on the Saturday evening following Thanksgiving and would be played in Akron's Rubber Bowl. The week of preparation began as usual with review of game film from the playoff against Toledo. On Thanksgiving, practice was scheduled for early in the morning so that everyone could enjoy the holiday, with schools obviously closed. That morning, we were drudging through plays and adjustments in a cold wind as a light snow started to fall from the typically gray skies. Feeling the mood and in an effort to fend off the cold, Joe Smith tried to get everyone who wasn't actually in the run-throughs to sing Christmas carols. You might expect that the coaches wouldn't appreciate it, but more players than expected joined in and everyone was amused by the short diversion. Maybe it was just the good spirits all around, because we were about to play for the state's first real championship, but Joe generally had a different sort of outlook on life and may have been one of the few people who could have gotten away with it. When we had taken the second team picture prior to entering the playoffs, each of us individually wrote down our names on cards. When the photo was released, we were all surprised to see that Joe had given his name as "JoJo Smith" and that is what it says in the legend of the photo anywhere it was printed. Maybe it was a pet name from one of the many girls he liked to talk about, but I think most of us simply thought that it was just another thing very much in line with what Joe would do.

The Rubber Bowl itself would have its grass field replaced with artificial turf the following year, but for the first championship game, it would be one of the final games played there on what remained of their grass field. It did not appear to be in pristine condition to start with, and that likely had as much to do with the plans to replace the field which were already in progress. Signs in several places inside the stadium said "Buy a piece of the turf." They were selling small souvenir squares of the artificial grass to help pay for the new field. But leading up to Saturday evening, it had rained off-and-on in Akron. Especially given the holiday, there was not a lot of opportunity to do thorough maintenance on the field, and it had already seen a full season of football by the University of Akron Zips. There had been about four inches of rain that month, with four-tenths of an inch of snow earlier that day. The wet and the cold had combined to make the field a wet, sloppy, muddy mess. The Raiders would play the game of their lives in the conditions with which they were most familiar, but everything about the game was slightly surreal. The conditions resulted in nearly every player quickly covered in mud and therefore unidentifiable to anyone who didn't know the person by sight rather than by number. We didn't use numbered jerseys in practice, so we knew each other by sight, often merely from differences in the type and style of facemask individuals players wore. Not only could most people in attendance not tell who was who, but because of the field conditions, neither school's band had been permitted to perform at halftime. Not long into the game, the public address announcer stated they did not know who was carrying the ball or making tackles, and subsequently made only brief pronouncements regarding the progress and any scoring when it was apparent (e.g. "second down and it looks like about six"). Newspaper and yearbook pictures from the day illustrate this well, but seldom identify who is actually in the picture. Co-captain Barry Simms was fortunate enough for the Warren's *Tribune Chronicle* to still read the "12" on his jersey through the mud and identify him in a picture shaking hands with Coach Novak toward the end of the game. Lest there be any suggestion of the playing conditions being the reason WWR won, it should be noted that Cincinnati Princeton is still, 50 years later, tied in fourth place for the record of having the most penalties in the history of the championship game.

Princeton actually scored first on the very first drive of the game. Their conversion failed, and thus took a 6-0 lead after just the first possession of the game. This may sound familiar, but those were the only points they would score in the entire game. A good return of Princeton's kickoff by Mike Spiva led to WWR's first score: a field goal. Junior Bill Williams, who had just a year earlier booted the first field goal in WWR history, would kick two that evening. Doing so means that Bill - to this very day fifty years later - is still in the record books, tied for the most field goals in the state championship game. Ross Browner later related that the first field goal looked close but that he had popped through the defense as it was kicked and was right in front of the official as the ball flew over the goalpost. He jumped up and down screaming "Yeah! Yeah!" with his arms upraised. Ross was amused because he said the referee looked like he wasn't quite sure whether it was good or not, but seeing Ross towering over him and yelling, he sheepishly raised his arms to signal that the kick was good.

It didn't really matter in the final analysis because, with Princeton beating themselves with penalties and WWR in control on both sides of the ball, they were in for a very long bus ride home to Cincinnati. The game simply was never even close. Mike Spiva ran for three touchdowns that day behind (my piggy-back partner) Jim King's blocking and a great offensive line. Later in the game, with things well in hand, Coach Novak began substituting players liberally into the game and even they scored a fourth touchdown. When the clock ran down, the very first Ohio Class AAA high school football championship had been won decidedly by Warren Western Reserve. The score was 37-6. We were in fact "Number One."

From the moment Joe Novak held that championship trophy on the muddy field in Akron, he knew that he had a lot of people to thank for all that had happened. A lot of things had gone on behind the spectacle of the game to make the victory possible. A number of people whose names will never be credited were instrumental in getting things done that had to be done on very short notice. We got the new equipment such as the Wilson footballs and the turf shoes, and found a place - any place with artificial turf - to practice. Assistant coaches travelled all over the state for days scouting teams that we might possibly have to play, all the while trying to calculate whether we even had a chance of getting into the playoffs. A great deal happened behind the scenes in just two weeks that November. Coach Novak tried his best to show his appreciation in interviews with reporters, at the Booster and Quarterback Club meetings, at the school celebration the following week, and to anyone who would listen when the subject seemed appropriate.

During the following school week, a formal celebration occurred in the jam-packed gymnasium, for which all of school had been excused to attend. Along with the band maintaining the fever pitch, multiple speakers were the order of the day with Coach Novak keynoting the event. Of course, he praised the players and the students' support and as expected, in his usual genial manner made the whole thing worth attending. Worth attending because significantly less can be said of the school board representatives who spoke first and literally harped at us, looking right at the football team in the front rows of the seats, chastising us over and over that we needed to have humility. I do not mean just a couple times, it was said over and over and over again. Everything else about their speeches was subdued and ironically *trite*. It was insulting because the entire team, the entire school, and the entire west side had been nothing but humble. It was insulting because the school had just done something that literally had never been done not only in its brief history, but also for the first time in the history of Ohio high school football. It was unquestionably and entirely an orderly – and deserved - *celebration*. What was the point then? These gentlemen, one of them in particular, had clearly decided in advance that this was an appropriate occasion to repeatedly make sure we knew our second class status in the city, at the precise time he should have been doing exactly the opposite. Gracious as ever and while thanking everyone in attendance, Coach Novak knew that speaking last gave him the last word, and he eloquently made sure everyone in the facility knew that this _was_ a big deal of which we should be proud, and commented that he had seen no one being anything but humble about it. We may have been thought of as river rats, but we were – undisputedly - the last rats standing[14].

*The first OHSAA Championship trophy sitting on
the counter in the school's main office.*

Change was coming. Coach Dick Lascola decided to leave. Whatever circumstances had led him to his decision, most of us knew we would be missing an important piece in the championship puzzle. However it transpired, he moved to California and ran a highly respected business focused upon the scouting of high school football players for colleges. Harry Beers took over as offensive coordinator, and a new running backs coach was hired. Even then, several of us thought that odd, rather than promoting someone familiar with our system from within. One of the more likely candidates however, Pat Guliano, had his sights on school administration, which he eventually achieved. Coach Guliano returned the following year as assistant coach for

---

[14] A reference to *Skyfall*; coincidentally a film which also celebrated a fiftieth anniversary of a sort.

the underclassmen, but had been instrumental as one of the coaches traversing Ohio to scout teams that we might eventually play if we made it into the playoffs.

Another change that Coach Novak was quick to share with us was that, as defending champions, we now had a huge target on our backs. We had been _the_ game every season for both Harding and for Austintown Fitch for a few years. Now, every team we played would have us marked on their schedule. We were reminded that we could not let our guard down in any game; that defending the title was just as hard as, or harder than winning it. It is likely that in the very least Class AA champions and our regular conference rival Akron St. Vincent thought they had something more to prove. As much as coaches harped on the need to work harder than ever, it never appeared that anyone was all the more concerned about any game or opponent than another, with the obvious exception of Harding. More or less, we approached the season in the same way we had the previous year. The reason we worked harder was to beat Harding. We were fairly certain they felt the same way about us.

Each year, all members of the team were given an athletic gray T-shirt with a slight variation for each school class. Seniors and juniors received a shirt that read, "Fighting Raider Varsity Football", with the word "Pride" inside a graphic football, depicted just above the word "Football." The sophomore shirts read, "Sophomore" instead of "Varsity", and "Desire" instead of "Pride." The freshman team shirts read, "Rookie" and "Win," correspondingly. This was virtually unchanging each year and a point of pride that you could wear to school whenever you liked. As school began in 1973, we received our varsity shirts and a second shirt that garnered a lot of wear. The second shirt read, "Defending 1972 State Champs" with "Raiders" inside the football graphic.

The more visible change was that the Varsity House was well under construction. We would soon be out of our concrete dungeon and into a multi-featured athletic facility, right next to the practice fields.

7

DEJA-VU

The Varsity House had been in the works for quite a while, but the timing made it seem as though it was a reward for winning the state championship. Truly however, that was just a coincidence. It may not have been the lap of luxury that modern sports teams enjoy, but it certainly seemed like it to us. The locker room and the lockers themselves were larger. Actually, everything was. This made functioning in the space much more comfortable. The coaches' office was finally of adequate size for the staff, and there was a separate dedicated training room with adjoining whirlpool bath. The latter was not the fancy resort amenity you might imagine, it was one of those galvanized washtub looking things with an attachment that swirled the water. Ever see the movie *Major League*? When James Gammon as the team Manager is finally fed up with the team owner's cutbacks because the whirlpool bath has no hot water? That's almost exactly what we had.

The equipment room was more than large enough for everything our football team required. Hard and fast rule: No one entered the equipment room except coaches or equipment managers. This was understood from the beginning, although I have no idea what might have happened if they had caught someone in there. I think they did let me in once to look for a different facemask, but I was of course, supervised. There wasn't really anything to tempt you with theft anyway, if that was the reason, but I understand boundaries had to be made and enforced.

The universal gym and all of the free weights and lifting stations were moved into designated workout and weight rooms. In the back of the facility was a meeting room with a white board (the school right next door still had chalkboards), which was large enough to hold the whole team when it was necessary. For the most part however, it was probably underused. We did use it to cover new formations for special teams, but not a lot else. My wife likes to ask people if they have ever been on television, because she discovered that a surprising number of people she meets or works with actually have been. The meeting room was the location of the first time that I was on television. One of Youngstown's TV station sports reporters came to the facility to do a feature on it just prior to an Open House which christened it. They corralled several of us into the meeting room and taped us pretending to have a meeting. Neal Hall, our starting halfback, hammed it up a bit in a clip by pretending to point out to the guy next to him something that wasn't even really on the board. The reporter appreciated it though, because the rest of us were all just sitting there, trying to pretend to be paying attention to ... nothing. During two-a-day lunch breaks, some guys would go in the room with the lights off and try to nap. Once, several guys came by as I was lying on the bench in front of my locker and asked me to tell Jim Browner when he came in that they were back there listening to Richard Pryor tapes. First, to be clear, it's likely we're talking 8-track tapes; not cassettes, and definitely not CDs or vinyl albums. What was different about 8-tracks wasn't just their size. It was because of the way the tape was wound into the cartridge, it could only be played in one direction. You could fast-forward (*well, forward slightly faster*) or click a button to change to the next track, but it was not possible to rewind. Four tracks were stacked on the tape in stereo, hence, two for each track or "8-track," so songs from an album were essentially stacked on top of each other. Second, I probably would have liked to come and listen with them, but I obligingly told Jim when he came in, who seemed to be headed that way anyway. I was relatively happy laying there listening to what was piped into the locker room. Occasionally they had a radio station on, but frequently guys brought in their tapes to play over the speaker system. Two that were used over and over (and over ...) were Edgar Winter's *They Only Come Out at Night*, featuring *Frankenstein* and Billy Preston's *Music is My Life* featuring *Will It Go Round in Circles*, both of which I heard literally dozens upon dozens of times that summer. With the speakers in the ceiling pointing down, the concrete floor and the nature of the metal fabrication of the walls, it made for an interesting and visceral listening experience. Until years later when I saw each of those guys play the songs live, I was convinced there was not a better way to hear them.

Coach Novak's handwritten note from our first team meeting in Varsity House.
I picked it out of the trash where he threw it afterward.
He actually talked about more than just attendance.

* * * * *

Because it didn't open until later in the summer of 1973, the Tuffy summer conditioning program began with the Varsity House still in its latter stages of completion, so initially we were still dependent upon the old locker room and weight stations. Since Jim King had graduated and although I actually was in considerably better physical condition than the year before, I had to find a new piggyback partner. I more wisely went with anyone that was closer to my size. There were more guys to pick from, as several new faces showed up who were hoping to join in the run for another championship. Ultimately, nearly every one of those new faces was gone before the end of two-a-days. Mainly, it was fellow returning split end Bill Taylor and I doubling up on the piggyback drill. We knew each other well.

The only problem I ever had with anyone on this team was for absolutely no reason other than one guy acting like a teenage punk. We were inside the school running the stairwells that summer when one of the linemen got it into his head that he was going to push me down the stairs. I never once had any interaction with him of any kind - ever. So to this day I'm convinced he was just being an idiot. First of all, this guy couldn't catch me on level ground if he was riding a bike. But in the landings between stories, people get bunched up, at which time he muscled his way through to get right behind me and shoved me in the back just as I took my first step. Luckily, the stairs were momentarily clear in the opposite direction, so I just leapt to the left over every step all the way to the landing, just barely clearing the final step. My only other choice would have been to fall forward and take out the four or five guys straight ahead of me. I got up quickly and cinched myself into the corner to turn around to let him pass, but he grabbed me by the arm thinking he could just throw me. He could not. Fortunately George Powell, who was our new starting quarterback, co-Captain, and his lifting partner was right behind him, saw what happening, grabbed *him* by the shirt and said only, "Let's go." He glared, but immediately obeyed George. I learned a lot about both of those guys that day. Later, during the season, George would often tap me to help him warm up his arm for practice, so he obviously had no issues and may have wondered at the time what that was all about, as much as I did. More than likely, George had seen him do something similar before. Coaches always harped to us to watch out for cheap shots during a game, such as late hits after the whistle and the like, but here was someone who was supposed to be a teammate trying to do just that.

Given the context, I would have had no problem whatsoever if someone really wanted, and had a reason, to tough it out in pads. But I was not about to be pushed down a flight of concrete and steel stairs just because some over-grown baby thought it might be funny. I had been hit and laid out by the best of them. Ross Browner once hit me so hard I literally landed on my head. I was on a scout team defense at safety, and Ross crossed over from his tight end spot to block me. Three or four guys watching the play said in unison, "Are you okay?" as I got up, curiously wondering why they were asking. Then I realized that I had a chunk of turf caught in the upper corner of my facemask and a big grass stain on the very top of my shoulder pad. But I went right back in.

When we picked up our helmets, cleats, pads and other equipment on August 14 in the gymnasium, we took our gear to a new locker in the Varsity House. Opening the House and starting two-a-days invited a special welcome from Coach Novak. In celebration of the beginning of the title defense and the Open House that had been scheduled for the community to see the new building, everything else in or around the facility had been freshly painted that weekend with metallic gold paint. It was not the bright yellow we were used to, it was metallic gold. So the goalposts, the cages, the blocking sled, and just about anything else that could be, except for the totem pole, were all gold. Coach Novak took this occasion to announce first to the team and then later in a welcoming speech at the Open House that "Everything has been painted gold ... and if it isn't gold, piss on it!" This was meant as both a point of pride for what had been accomplished and symbolic of the team as a whole, as much as it was a dig at the cross-town team's objectionable red. At his earlier welcoming for team members, he jokingly added, "The only thing not painted gold is the grass. And if you piss on that, it will turn gold!" As far as I know, no one took him seriously and what grass there was that season remained green.

It was during the first week of two-a-days that I got my first football-related concussion. We were still practicing from the standpoint that the running game would dominate our play calling, so over and over again, the ends traded off blocking each other as a safety or as a linebacker. We didn't have a full formation, it was just us, and therefore it was a matter of where the defender was placed. As each split end took his turn running at the defender and throwing a block, the defender went to the back of the line, and the one who had just thrown the block became the defender. When it was my turn, I ran head-to-head into Bill Taylor and immediately started seeing double. That wasn't so bad, but what I remember most about it was that the double vision affected my balance. I have since had other concussions, including a couple much worse, but I still believe that there is no such thing as a mild concussion, although comparatively, that's what I would call this one. The trainer sauntered over, told me to sit down, handed me some smelling salts, and then just left. Once again, he could not be bothered. When I started seeing correctly, I went back into practice, but by that time, we had moved on to some activity other than smacking each other in the head. It happened once again a week or two later, and once again, I was given smelling salts and a brief break. Fortunately for Nick Amorganos, the trainer was marginally more useful in providing medical assistance when later that season Nick broke his leg during a JV game. And that was despite Nick screaming at him not to touch him - actually screaming at him repeatedly in misery, "Don't touch me! I'll kill you!" But Nick got the attention he needed until an ambulance came. He recovered from the break and played defensive tackle the following year.

During the first week or two after classes started, I stopped into the yearbook office to see my friend Doug Dill who was by then an officer of some kind on the staff. While I was waiting, I saw some pictures on the table and flipped through them. One of the student photographers had come to football practice and took several photos of the team, all of which were black and white. But just as my attention was drawn to what I thought was an excellent photo, the lead photographer also happened to walk into the small office. I turned to tell Doug, "Hey, this is a great picture," by which I was inferring that they should use it in the yearbook, but the lead photographer piped in, "Yeah, it's too bad no one knows who it is." To which I immediately replied, "That's Lanny." He said, "Huh?" So I added, "That's Lanny McElrath and it's a great picture." He asked indignantly, "How could you possibly know that's him?" We did not have numbers on our summer mesh practice jerseys, and numbers, he assumed, was the only way to tell each player apart. I tried to explain that I knew who everyone was in every picture they had right there on the table, because I knew everyone by sight. This guy's family happened to own the local camera store (*Remember those?*), so he was convinced from an early age that he knew absolutely everything there was to know about photography. Everything except apparently, what or who it actually was every time he released the shutter to photograph something. He got irate, irrationally quickly, at which time both Doug and another guy on the staff interrupted him. Both of them told him they were sure I was right, and tried again to explain how I knew so easily who the guys in the pictures were. He got even more upset and just left. They never used that picture or any of the others in that pile, a couple others of which were also pretty good. Whether it still exists, which is unlikely, there once was a picture of Lanier McElrath during cage drills, getting set to take on a teammate who was out of frame. It really was a great photo. Because it was at practice, it was taken close-up, framed and focused, with the new paint on the cages glistening in the sunlight. It should have been used in the yearbook ... or in the very least, given to him. Sorry Lanny, I tried.

We began the season once again at home shutting out Cleveland Collinwood. But just before that game, we as a team were faced with a very unusual situation. Burrell McGhee had been one of the rotating regulars at split end the prior season. However, Burrell also played basketball and was clearly built for the sport.

When the 1972-73 basketball season ended, he made it known that he was concentrating on basketball, and therefore giving up football. He did not attend a single session of spring conditioning, summer Tuffy, or a single day of August football practice because of this decision. Perhaps a little too coincidentally however, just days before school started and our first game of the year, he went to Coach Novak and asked if he could rejoin the team. One has to believe that any other coach at the time would have simply and quickly made the decision and resolved the matter right then and there, but instead Coach Novak told Burrell that he would ask the team how we felt about it and then let him know. It was absolutely the correct thing to do, yet another example of Coach Novak's consummate leadership skills. He knew we as a team had to live with it, so it needed to be our decision, not his. Every single member of the team was given a piece of paper and asked to write either 'yes' or 'no' and the coaches would count the votes. When the votes were counted, Coach came out of the office visibly beside himself with second thoughts: it was a tie. He told Burrell that he would discuss it with the team and take a second vote, but when Burrell found out that essentially half of the team had voted no, he told Coach Novak not to bother. The interesting thing about the entire episode is that afterward I never once heard a single person comment on the matter or boast which way they had voted, as so many are wont to do. Burrell did concentrate on basketball - well enough to win a scholarship to the University of Michigan. He transferred after a year or two to Kent State where he subsequently held numerous school records in the sport for years. Unfortunately, Burrell ultimately became what was probably the first member of the 1972 championship team to pass away, a victim of gun violence.

After Collinwood, we travelled to Austintown to play Fitch. My cousin was a senior there and during the prior weekend we happened to stop over for a visit. Actually it was probably for Wedgewood Pizza - down the street from Fitch is the best pizza in all of Ohio - it's still there today! But one of his friends who started for them at tailback happened to be there. He started to mention something about the game coming up at which my cousin quickly made sure, "He plays for Reserve, you know?" I could literally see the wheels turning in his head, he desperately wanted to make an inappropriate and in all likelihood racist comment, but wisely thought the better of it. After a little friendly banter, we changed the subject and moved on to doing something else. Just days later, I ran over to him to shake his hand as he was about to enter their locker room at the end of the game. He later admitted to my cousin that he appreciated the gesture, but at the time, wasn't really in the mood because of the final score.

Barberton, who had always played us tough, followed next, and then Struthers, which was another of the many incorporated suburbs of Youngstown. In the fourth quarter of the Struthers game, our starting halfback Neal Hall had somehow sweet-talked one of our defensive backs into letting him play his position. He did this presumably because he wanted to repay them with a few of the hits they had been giving him, but honestly, sometimes you just never knew where Neal was coming from in his thinking. When he realized Neal was in there, Coach Novak suddenly became irate, "What the hell's he doing in there?!" Instantly because I happened to be standing there, he pushed me on the shoulder pad and yelled, "Get Neal outta there, NOW!" Coach was more than a little mad. He did not want his starting halfback risking any kind of injury on a lark. That's the only time I know of that something like that happening, but sometimes goofy stuff just happened. Once, one of our linebackers seeing a replacement coming into the huddle and calling to him that he was being substituted, ran to the opposing team's sideline to get off the field for no other reason than he was closer to it. This immediately resulted in a penalty. I know Neal didn't try his ploy again, because he got an earful when he got back to the sideline. The stern lecture was probably a good thing though, because Neal ultimately finished the regular season with over 1,000 yards rushing – something that hadn't been done in Warren since 1959. Who did that, you might ask? A Harding halfback and future NFL Hall-of-Famer named Paul Warfield.

In the end, we had won our first four games by a combined score of 90-14, including two shutouts. Our rivalry with Harding was next. Unfortunately, Harding had stubbed its toes, so the rivalry game would yet again be denied the storybook tale of two undefeated teams. Harding would eventually finish their season with a 6-4 record. The cross-town rivalry was however, once again a sell-out. And once again, it would be a closely fought battle. Despite exchanges of punts and overall stubborn defense from both teams, a run by halfback Neal Hall put WWR up 7-0 at halftime. With Neal's speed, we used more I-formation sets that year, since that formation behind the line gave him addition fractions of a second to find the best block to follow or choose the best running lane. We really did do fairly well during games on special teams for the most part, despite not spending a lot of time in practice on it. We had blocked a Harding punt the previous year to set up a score, so perhaps we just felt obliged to return the favor. Harding managed to block Ed's punt and ended up with six points on the board. Their new Head Coach, Ed Glass, decided to go for the two-point conversion after the score, but that attempt was squashed. Both teams were clearly playing to win. Realizing the game was clearly going to be a low scoring contest, Glass undoubtedly felt compelled to try for two points – and a possible win – when the opportunity presented itself.

Shortly after the Harding score, however, the Raider offense started moving and scored a second touchdown on a pass from quarterback George Powell to sophomore Willard Browner. Willard was Browner brother number three on Raider teams within the prior two seasons. He started at halfback in the role vacated when John Hickman graduated and would do so for three straight seasons until he followed both of his brothers to Notre Dame. The extra point was good, and WWR was ahead 14-6. With more drives stalled by tough defense on both sides, that's how the game ended. We were 5-0 and very happy with the victory, but there was not the same jubilation as last year because we were not avenging a prior year loss this time, and our sights had immediately shifted at the final gun from beating Harding to getting into the playoffs.

The remaining five games of the scheduled season were all won by shut-out. The score total for those five games was 112-0. The game immediately following Harding, however, was a nail-biter. From the time we started preparing for Youngstown Cardinal Mooney, we were made exceedingly aware that they had one of the best running backs in the state. Whether or not this was how Ted Bell happened to play for Mooney, it was well known at the time that Catholic high schools in Ohio could do what public schools could not. Effectively, they could recruit players. With public schools, you were required to attend the school (elementary, junior high, high school) designated by each city or county school district according to your home address. Being private, Catholic high schools could accept students from virtually anywhere within a reasonable distance. The well-known Moeller High School in Cincinnati would later be suspected of unfairly recruiting players who could not otherwise afford to attend the school. This speculative fodder had likely manifested because of Moeller's succession of winning football seasons.

The actual matter is neither here nor there, because we would play Mooney and Mooney not only had Ted Bell but also had a bunch of other guys that made them a good team. If we expected to return to the playoffs, Mooney was the next team standing in our way. Our mimeographed (*Ahh, remember the smell?*) scouting report for Mooney that week deviated from the usual. Virtually every other time, the reports ran down each opposing offense or defense player's pluses and minuses with comments such as "Runs off tackle well", "Good Blocker", etc. For Ted Bell, the scouting report read, "Mr. Everything. Is one of the finest if not the best back in the County, State, U.S.A." In the diagram of their offense, every player is listed only by last name next to the circle with his number and place in their formation. Bell was listed as "Mr. Ted Bell." Similarly, their defensive concern for us, left inside linebacker Mark Malie might be interested to know that our scouting report comments regarding him read, "A̲ BITCH ... great versus run."

Mooney was also atypical. Their quarterback was left handed, so they favored running and throwing to the left offensive side a little more than to the right which most teams did. Most teams, including Mooney, were defensively stronger on the left side, to defend most teams' offensive right-side emphasis.

CARDINAL MOONEY OFFENSE

#85 – RE – Bob Sammartino – 6'3" – 225 – Sr.
    Mostly used as a blocker. Not a real threat on pass. He will hold if he starts to slip off a block. Very strong.

#71 – RT – Rich Marisco – 6'1" – 210 – Sr.
    Big, strong and quick. Comes off ball very well and delivers a good forearm. Also a good pass blocker.

#66 – RG – Tim Fyda – 6'1" – 180 – Jr.
    Has good technique. Doubles well. Not real fast. Executes well.

#53 – C – Bill Thornton – 6'1" – 210 – Sr.
    Fairly slow off ball but very strong. Sustains like hell!! Executes well.

#64 – LG – Mike Lodyn – 5'10" – 195 – Sr.
    Good technique when trapping Executes "Tom" well. Very good blocker-strong. Executes well.

#82 – LT – Brian Cicuto – 5'11" – 190 – Sr.
    Good agility, fair size, will sustain well.

#80 – LE – Rich Yssh – 6'0" – 180 – Sr.
    Good blocker-double teams well. Excellent receiver. Fine speed. Likes to throw-play action passes to him.

#16 – QB – Dave Lockshaq – 5'10" – 165 – Sr.
    Fine quarterback. Extends his faker well to backs. Likes to run on the belly option. Will throw to backs, fair passer.

#22 – UP Back – Ron Pasquale – 5'10" – 165 – Sr.
    Good blocker, will kick end out on passes and isolates well. Will not carry ball. Is like a guard.

#33 – FB – Dave Handel – 5'10" – 175 – Sr.
    Tough kid, runs belly well. Likes to run over people. Arm tackling will not bring him down.

#20 – TB – Ted Bell – 6'1" – 185 –Sr.
    Mr. Everything. Is one of the finest if not the best back in the County, State, U.S.A. Will break plays wide that should be run wide. Runs sweep and power well.

Scouting report on Youngstown Cardinal Mooney's offense,
including "Mr. Everything," Ted Bell.

CARDINAL MOONEY DEFENSE

#62 - R DE - Bob Carney - 5'10" - 172 - Sr.
    Is not crashing 4-4 end. Reads keys well. Can be sealed in on his move.

#84 - R OLB - Tom Fabiny - 6'1" - 170 - Jr.
Plays pass well. Exceptionally quick. Good on fires. Comes up quick on run prone
pass defense.

#81 - E - Mike Lokey - 5'11" - 180 - Sr.
    Not great size but plays run well. Uses hands well to play off blockers.

#63 - L LB - Jeff Johnson - 5'10" - 180 - Jr.
    Tough kid. Plays run well. Drops off in long yardage situations.
    Will rush pass his way, must block him well.

#32 - LT - Jody McColloh - 6'2" - 205 - Jr.
    Very quick, strong inside forearm.

#51 - LILB - Mark Malie - 5'10" - 210 - Jr.
    A BITCH--strong forearms and hand shiner, great versus run.

#50 - RILB - Charles Peace - 5'10" - 190 - Jr.
    Pressures well on scrape when roll to his side, fair speed.

#70 - RT - Kevin Tomasko - 6'0" - 190 - Sr.
    Good strength, but slow.

#16 -   - Dave Lockshaw - 5'10" - 165 - Sr.
    Strong side H.B. Tough boy. Likes to come up on run. Plays pan well. Lines
    up 7 yds. off ball.

#80 - Rich Yash - 6'0" - 180 - Sr.
    Lines up 12 yds. deep and plays the field. Covers deep well. He likes
    to come up on run.

#21 - Mel Anderson - 5'10" - 165 - Sr.
    Weak side H.B. Has fine speed-plays 6 yds. off ball. Will squirm on
    ball action.

*Scouting report on Youngstown Cardinal Mooney's defense. These reports
were distributed to the team before we played them in week six, and then
once again for the 1973 championship game. They were unique in their
praise of players' abilities, especially regarding Ted Bell and Mark Malie.*

This was the game and the team for which we favored a more aggressive defensive philosophy called "Iron 8 Tight." Joe Smith would move up near the line from his typical position farther behind in the defensive backfield as a safety. He became what many teams referred to as a Monster backer, a strong safety who was effectively a roving third linebacker. This placed eight men at the defensive line, hence the term "Iron 8 Tight." Despite his slimmer build, Joe was very effective at hitting and tackling larger ball carriers. Because he was a roving defender, he shadowed Bell's movements from the hike of the football. Part of Joe's responsibility was to remind Mr. Ted Bell that he was in our sights. He was to do this by hitting him – legally – on every play that he could, whether he was the ball carrier or not. Because he was to shadow Bell, he likely increased his opportunity to be in on the tackle if nothing else. In practice, he initially and matter-of-factly moved up on the defensive left, until coaches recalled Mooney's backside emphasis and placed Joe as a middle stand-up defender, behind and between our two linebackers, or to the right side, depending on Mooney's formation. If Mooney was snugged up and balanced, both cornerbacks were to move up as well.

IRON EIGHT TIGHT

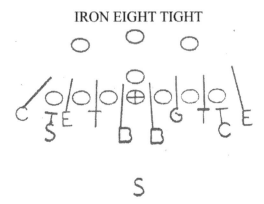

The game was a seemingly never ending series of stalled drives and punts on both sides. If a low scoring, defensive battle is your idea of a great football game, this one would have been one for the ages. The difference became a matter of effective scouting and coaching. Mooney started a sustained drive and was well into Raider territory pressing toward the north goal. As they ran an option play to their left, Bell ended up on the ground from a hard tackle and the ball came loose, whereupon Raider right defensive end Brian DeCree picked up the football and ran almost 70 yards down the sideline for a touchdown. He was in the correct position, as his responsibility was preventing the runner from getting outside of him, when the ball trailed off and onto the ground right in front of him. The conversion failed and the game eventually ended 6-0; the fumble return being the only score of the game. We were pleased to have won, but there was not the usual elation with the victory. We had just gone toe-to-toe with a formidable and equally matched opponent. In the film reviews Coach Novak praised Brian, but emphasized that we had been lucky. While I do not disagree, I believe Louis Pasteur's oft repeated quote, "Chance favors the prepared mind" better sums up the outcome. We were victorious because Mooney had been well scouted and we were well prepared for what they would do and how they would do it. This was an archetype example of the notion that games can be and occasionally are won by what happens off the field as well as on. The coaches who were responsible for preparing the team for "the finest if not the best back in the County, State, U.S.A." should have gotten the award that week.

Perhaps it woke us up, or perhaps we were just much more evenly matched with Mooney, but the remaining four games on our schedule we won much more comfortably. The final four games had a combined score of 106-0. The closest game was a 12-0 victory over Cuyahoga Falls in the ninth game of the year. It was a very cold evening, and Falls had a decent team on both sides of the ball. The fact that we shut them out was coincidental. They played us tough and gained some momentum when our offense uncharacteristically fumbled, perhaps due in part to how cold it was. In another bit of karma, this happened on the very first play, a matter of seconds after we had recovered one of their fumbles. Ponce Henderson had barely gotten back to the bench to take a breather when several of us yelled for him to go back on defense. He kept looking at everyone nearby saying, "What? What happened?" repeatedly as he ran back to the huddle while the offense retreated back to the sidelines. I don't blame him, it happened so quickly, but the defense held again, and Falls was shut out. The game was bitter cold and windy and Ed Manusakis was one of the few players who managed to wrangle a team overcoat as minimal protection from the weather. He told me to stick by him, so that when he was in for defense or punts, I could wear it until he came back out. This sounded like a good deal to me because there just weren't enough of them. I doubt there were more than two dozen and coaches wore some of them. The majority of players did not have one. So it was a good deal: I got warmer and I kept the jacket warm for Ed, while Ed knew the coat was secured from losing it to someone else. He and I also had a friendly rivalry going during the 40-yard wind sprints that we ran almost every session once Tuffy started in the summer and all through the season. There was no animosity between us, just a friendly "I'm gonna win this one" each and every time. And that was a lot of wind sprints.

Once again, in the days before our final scheduled game against Lorain Southview, Senior Hit fever infected the team. Unlike the year before, some names were being passed around freely. Early in the week, probably on Tuesday, a teammate came up to me and said, "Hey! You know Ponce is picking you?" I just said, "Whatever," even though I wondered what was up with that. I had gotten to know Ponce Henderson better on a field trip that spring. I had a great deal of respect for him, so part of me was flattered that he'd waste his pick on me, while the other part of me knew how hard he hit people and that made me a little apprehensive. Mostly, I thought it was a joke and that he was probably just teasing me a little, maybe even a few of us. In truth however, he had once quite deliberately punched me in the nose during practice. I was on a scout team as a tight end on the right side, opposite to him at defensive end. I think it was just too easy for him to resist. I was looking down rather than up as I should have been, and he saw that the gap in my facemask was perhaps bigger than it should have been. So in his way of telling me, at "Set" he demonstrated it to me by slamming his fist through the gap and quite literally punching me in the nose. First I was stunned, but then I thought it was funny. I even jokingly wrote about it later as part of another English class assignment. And yes, I tried to have my facemask adjusted, but there wasn't much they could do without drilling new holes in the side of the helmet for the fasteners that held the facemask in place. So, I just tried to make sure that I kept my head up.

To my surprise, I think it was the next day after the teammate had said something, I was watching a drill and waiting my turn as Ponce walked up to me with a sly grin, "Heyyy, Jim." I smiled back and said only, "I heard," and we both just started laughing. I figured I would just straight up ask him, "You're gonna waste your pick on me?" "Well, you know ..." was all he said. I guess he was going to pick someone, and I was as good a choice as any. As it happened, either that day after practice or the next, several seniors became over-zealous thinking about Senior Hit and took a few guys out and roughed them up. I didn't see it, and do not know who was involved, but as I got dressed, Willie Lewis literally staggered into the locker room, covered with mud. He had been pressed face down into one of the many muddy puddles with which we were all too familiar, as it was imprinted all over his face. He was trying to give his trademark smile, but couldn't bring himself to do it. He seemed to be in a bit of shock and had trouble forming coherent words. Just then I heard some other guys screaming and still don't know what that was all about, but clearly Willie wasn't the only one who had been ambushed. Long story short: The co-Captains were summarily called into the coaches' office and told that the seniors had overstepped their bounds. There would be no Senior Hit.

Interestingly enough, the coaches came up with another plan. Instead of the sacrificial offering that was Senior Hit, they would make a new contest: backs vs. linemen. The coaches took two of the blocking dummies and laid them parallel just a couple feet apart, creating a narrow path between them. There was no choosing on anyone's part. The coaches called out two players: one back and one lineman, and each time they were matched purposefully. The two players laid flat on their backs head-to-head between the dummies. At the whistle each man jumped up from the prone position to either a) as the back carrying the ball, break any tackle attempt and get past the lineman to "score," or b) as the lineman, tackle the back within the short, narrow path. Both players had to stay within the boundaries set by the blocking dummies. In other words, you had to flip over, orient yourself, and go straight at each other. Unlike Senior Hit, there wasn't really any building up of steam, you both just flipped over and were barely more than a step apart. It was all bragging rights and letting off steam, nobody actually "won" anything. The first few challenges were clearly thought through by the coaches, because they made sure that a few people in particular were matched up against each other. They did not take junior or senior class into consideration; they simply called two names who were to be challengers. This was right up Larry Mallory's alley. He wasn't the only one, but he definitely liked the contact part of football, and cheered outrageously each time a lineman won his bout, or even if there was just any solid contact between the players.

Despite the closed spaces, there were several impressive hits, and a couple bad ones, where the back simply and easily broke a tackle attempt. We did several of these, and then Coach Novak, said something to the effect, "Okay, that'll do it. Everybody happy?" This is why I believe the drill was intended to teach the team or a couple players in particular, a lesson. Because he really wasn't pressing to have everyone do it. He more or less read off his list of combatants and figured that was good enough. If there had been scoring, the linemen would have roundly won, but I don't think Coach Novak cared who won or lost, he just wanted the aggression that had resulted in cancelling Senior Hit addressed on the field, in pads. But just then Jim Browner spoke right up, "James ain't gone yet!" pointing at me. True, I hadn't, but neither had a lot of others. Let's see: as an end, technically I was a lineman, but defensively, I was a back. It didn't matter, because it was clear to me that tackling the guy was the better choice, so I jumped right in on the ground on that side, while Coach picked someone else to be the back and gave him a ball. As I was lying there, all I kept thinking was, *Which way should I roll when I jump up; to the right or left?* - as if that mattered. There wasn't really enough time to think, so at the whistle all I did was react. Either we both rolled in opposite directions or the other guy was already trying to skirt by along one side, because we were at a very slight angle once we were up and facing each other. I tried to plant my foot as best I could and went straight at him, and with a big crack of the pads went right down: tackled him in place. Larry, who was rooting for a good hit as well as cheering for the linemen, immediately yelled out, "AW-RIGHT CAREY! STUCK 'IM GOOD!!" He was so into it, he grabbed me by the back of my shoulder pads while I was still on the ground and lifted me up to congratulations by the other linemen. It turned out that everyone was getting so hyped and enjoying the contest so much that they made sure everyone took a turn at it. A lot of us much preferred this to standing helplessly as someone charged at you from five yards away. This kind of one-on-one contest gave everyone had a chance to show their mettle.

Practice goes on for three months, so the memory of one session can dissolve into another, even at the time we were doing it. You get so familiar with the sounds of the game and of practice that you take them for granted. A play started with Coach Novak giving Barry or George the play to call in the huddle, with the inevitable exhortation, "Run it!" There would be some mumbling in the huddle as the QB called the play and then in unison, a hand clap, as everyone said "Break" or "Block" or a combination of the two. At the line the defense would see the formation and the lineman would see where defenders were placed, at which point the line captain would give a signal, typically "Rule!" as the defense called out one of many line and secondary signals just before our quarterback yelled, "Down!" and "Set!" At "Set," a maelstrom of oofs and arghs and grunts along with the sounds of plastic helmets and pads colliding all reverberated together as the play unfolded. When the runner got through the line, or was tackled, or the pass was caught, the whistle blew just as it would in a game, at which point everyone headed back to the huddle. So day in and day out, running many of the same plays over and over, we heard these sounds as an ongoing rhythm; a soundtrack to our football existence. We got very used to the sounds and essentially tuned them out – until and unless, like a singer improvising different words to a well-known song, the sound changed.

The later it was in the season, the more comfortable Coach Novak was with the first team offense practicing pass plays against a live scout defense. Once in particular, I was throwing a football back and forth with someone on the sideline to stay active, when in my subconscious I heard Coach again say "Run it!" I heard the huddle break. I heard "Down" and "Set." I heard the grunts and "arghhh's from the linemen executing blocks. And then, the sound of nothing alerted me. I wondered ... where's the whistle? I didn't hear a whistle. A few more seconds went by, and then I heard Coach Novak screaming at the absolute top of his lungs, "CATCH .. THE DAMN .. FOOTBAAALL!!" Today, it's just hilarious; it's one of my best memories of those endless practices. At the time however, my first thought was, 'Put me in, I'll catch it,' which was replaced in a nanosecond with the thought, 'Wow, is he mad.' I had never and would not ever again see or hear Coach Novak as mad as he was at that moment. No one said a word, not even the other coaches.

The offense huddled back up as Coach was still aggravated and while not actually calling the play just yelled, "Run it again!" This time I watched the play as Don Henderson caught the ball, the whistle blew, and there was a visible sigh of relief from the entire team. I hesitate to give Don's name, because I do not actually know who the ball was throw to on the previous play, since we would simulate game conditions by rotating players – and the play – into the huddle each time. So I don't know who it was that dropped the ball, or more correctly, the succession of dropped balls. I do think our scout defense had backed off ever so slightly, so that whoever the ball was thrown to would have a clean opportunity to catch it. The offense had the spotlight, everyone's attention was focused breathlessly on them running the play and catching the ball. In any case, there must have been multiple unsuccessful pass plays, probably to different receivers before Coach Novak blew his top as he did that day.

The regular season wound down with another shutout victory over Lorain Southview. In his pre-game speech, Coach Novak knew it was the last home game, and the last time seniors would be in Mollenkopf Stadium dressed to play a football game. He called on everyone to appreciate the tradition that WWR had built in such a short history, and that we now represented and were part of that tradition. He asked us to play not for ourselves, but for the players who had built that winning tradition in just the prior seven seasons, and to drive it home, he named several of the guys' older brothers just to make the game more personal for everyone. Perhaps I remember it because he did not do that before the last home game in 1972, and because I now wish he had saved that speech for our last playoff game. As WWR again finished undefeated in the regular season, the coaches awaited a call from OHSAA officials. They were a little more certain this time that we were in, but as always, nothing was official until teams were notified. We soon found that WWR had won Region 1 for the second year, by a margin of nearly 6% over Willoughby in second place. Harding, although finishing the season with a 6-4 record, was in eighth place (of 67 places). This still seems unlikely. Given their four losses, the six teams that Harding did beat must have done quite well against everyone else they played, because Harding had a sizable jump in standings because of third level points. WWR would play Bowling Green, at the Akron Rubber Bowl in the first playoff round - this time on their new artificial turf.

The other two Class AAA teams in the playoffs would play their semi-final round at the University of Cincinnati's Nippert Stadium. There, local favorite Cincinnati Moeller would play Region 3 winner ... Youngstown Cardinal Mooney.

8

BELL

Here might very well be the moment in time where the issue or conflict began that led the OHSAA to change how schools were chosen for playoff spots. Mooney, with a 9-1 record, won Region 3 over perennial poll favorite Massillon. Massillon at 8-1-1 was less than 6 total points behind Mooney, which amounted to only 8/10ths of 1 percent. There does not appear to have been any undefeated teams in Region 3 in 1973. Note the phrase "total points." In this, just the second year of the playoff system, teams in each region were ranked on the total of first, second, and third level points combined, just as they were the year before. Every year hereafter, starting in 1974 and continuing today, teams are ranked – and therefore chosen for a playoff spot – by a total of first and second points only.

So what, you might ask? If ranking had been by first and second level points in 1973, Massillon - not Mooney - would have been in the semi-final game against Moeller. It would also have made a huge difference for smaller Class A high school Gibsonburg, who would have soundly won their region over Montpelier. But it was Montpelier who went to the playoffs based on the total of first, second, and third level points. One must ask: Why did they suddenly change the ranking system? A hint at the reason comes with the certainty that it wasn't Gibsonburg that had the clout, following, winning history, or political influence to effect such change.

Acknowledging that it is entirely possible that Massillon still might have lost to Moeller in the semi-final game, the system nonetheless took away the third and final remote possibility for WWR to face off against Massillon in a span of just 15 months. Massillon team backers must also have realized that they were once again denied a chance to play WWR - something both teams' supporters appear to have coveted. As an academic researcher, it is necessary to restate that including the third level points should in fact be the correct way to rank teams. This is effectively proven by the fact that *it actually made a difference as to which teams got in* – both in 1972 and 1973 - and that quantified difference does in fact represent 'strength of schedule.' This was Jack Harbin's intent all along, whether or not it was OHSAA's. So in that vein, there is no objection to the historical outcome. A clear objection would be to that of the arbitrary change. Why did the OHSAA drop the third level points to rank teams the following year? Someone had to decide that third level points were to be used solely in the event of a tie. To clarify further, the OHSAA also stopped reporting those third level points. We no longer know what the state's actual calculations for third level points are. But they exist – because they are calculated in case of a tie. Rhetorical Question: Why might they do that? Rhetorical Answer: To stop speculation and complaints about the outcomes. After two years, they were no longer concerned with ties, and as a result, even less concerned with providing complete information to the public. A demonstrable consequence of those decisions was that they were no longer as concerned with accuracy.

If you're wondering if three levels is better, then why not go with four, the answer is diminishing marginal returns. It would require more work, in some aspects more than just a little, tracking matchups just one additional level, even though most of the final scores necessary for the calculations would already be recorded. As a matter of speculation, it is entirely possible, perhaps likely, that additional levels are already tracked for research purposes, but not acknowledged. Some, especially when Ohio schools play teams in neighboring states, would require broader tracking, which would in all likelihood lead to additional sampling error. The latter are points of missing or incorrect data, here and there. That's just the nature of increasing the volume of data points exponentially or outside of data reporting standards. This would also happen because information or data points increase significantly with each level. So the net result really is that beyond three levels, it is likely you would be getting very little new information, and nothing that would make a difference. As related earlier, Harbin's system effectively requires a three-step process and three levels are enough to rank teams based on their strength, which was and is the entire point. The importance of third level points is that they provide an indication of how good the ten teams that Team A played are, something that second level win-loss records alone cannot do.

But from 1974 onward, the OHSAA's rankings are based on first and second level points only.

* * * * *

I walked to the Varsity House from home around lunch time on Sunday to see if anyone was there and if they had heard anything. Approaching the building, Coach Beers saw me coming and said, "We're in. We play Bowling Green." At the team meeting on Monday, Coach Novak was in a great mood. We were in the playoffs. We had also, quite notably, been named the AP poll State Champions, something that with certainty would not have happened if we had not won the playoff championship the year before. By the time of our team meeting Monday afternoon, preparations had already been made. Since the Rubber Bowl had a new artificial surface, we would practice one day later in the week at Baldwin Wallace once again. Coach Novak also told us that he had told the official who had called that he didn't care what roster restriction they wanted, he was bringing everyone on the team and would provide everyone's name to them. That was around 52 players, which included only a couple sophomores, but not the entire sophomore team, which is what really had complicated the issue the year before.

About this time, Ed Manusakis went around the Varsity House locker room one day with what appeared to be a pristine new football. He had every one on the team sign it, and he was meticulously insistent upon it. He wanted each of us to sign it and he wanted it done right then and there. I assumed at the time that he was keeping it for himself, but he may have had another purpose, I really don't know. Whatever his purpose, I thought it was a great idea, but I always assumed he had it displayed somewhere as a memento of those days.

Practice went smoothly in the days leading up to our Baldwin Wallace session. When we arrived at the campus outside of Cleveland, we were ushered off the school busses and directly into the stadium seats. The Browns were still using the field and as the only spectators there, we got to watch them for almost an hour. Among others, there was running back Leroy Kelly and Don Crockroft, another straight on kicker with a square-toed shoe. Quarterbacking was Mike Phipps, the guy they had traded Paul Warfield away to get. It literally was just all business for them, and then they just summarily left the field as a group. We used a different locker room, but still had to wait until they had vacated the field to go change into our uniforms for some reason. Initially, we spent some time just getting the feel of it, planting our feet and making cuts back and forth; just running around with our turf shoes. The surface was uniformly level; there seemed to be little variation in the length or size of the blades of fake grass. Practice went well and we worked more than usual on the kicking game, since the field surface would have a different feel for our kickers as well. By the time the light was fading, it was time to go. Next up would be WWR's second trip to the state playoffs.

The field at the Rubber Bowl was a thing to behold. The mud was gone. It was new artificial turf: level, smooth, and a vivid green. Maybe just because it was newer, the field looked and felt more like real grass. It was so new that as we ran over it, sprigs of plastic grass popped loose from the turf here and there, just as bits of shag often come off newly laid carpet. Between warmups and returning to the field for the game from the locker room, what little light there was had gone, the wind had picked up, and it was one of those classically cold fall evenings in northeast Ohio. It eventually turned almost bitterly cold, although no one on the field seemed to mind.

Before the game started, a game official inadvertently told Coach Novak that it was time to take the field. We all jumped up and ran onto the field, only to find that something wasn't quite right. The band was still on the field. We had barely reached the sidelines when the P.A. system asked everyone to rise for the national anthem. For the first and only time ever, we were on the field and doffing our helmets to stand in line as the band played the Star Spangled Banner. If for some reason we weren't psyched up enough by that point, the anthem did it. The brisk air, the bright lights, the band playing - the importance of the event became overriding. As the crowd cheered the end of the anthem, we were ready.

Actually, we were probably a little too ready. All of the excitement led to some jitters, but fortunately not to any mistakes. After the first quarter while the two teams were getting used to each other, it was still a scoreless ballgame. Early in the second quarter WWR sustained a drive that ended with a Bill Williams field goal. We had scored first. Shortly before the half, another drive resulted in a touchdown. With the conversion good, we took a 10-0 lead into halftime. As in the semi-final game the previous year, adjustments were quickly made on both offense and defense. We still had Bud Myers as defensive coordinator, but since Coach Lascola had left, Harry Beers took charge of coordinating the offense. Our defense had been holding Bowling Green well, and Coach Beers' adjustments worked very well on offense. The game went from a closely fought first half to a Raider wave that washed over Bowling Green in the second half. The game effectively became entirely one-sided after Brian DeCree blocked a Bowling Green punt. He literally just breezed past everyone from his end spot, getting to the punter almost as soon as the ball did. It actually seemed as though he had to hesitate momentarily or he would have overrun the ball before it was kicked. He barely had to raise his arms, because he was right there, in front of the punter's leg. The blocked punt itself seemed to take the wind out of their sails, but the quick touchdown WWR made out of the block really iced it. The offense just rolled after that, scoring an additional two touchdowns before the fourth quarter even started. Up 30-0 as the final quarter began, Coach Novak started substituting liberally. One reason was that he wanted to give more of the team some playoff experience, and another was that he did not want to appear to be running up the score by continuing to use the first team players. Literally everyone played that day. At some point late in the fourth quarter, Coach Novak decided that he wanted Joe O'Grady to have a pass reception. He called the same pass play three times in a row, but the ball never made it to Joe, or actually, to anyone else. Our backup quarterback only knew the play relayed into him, he did not know that he was supposed to look for or throw it to Joe. I think Coach may have even just yelled to the huddle "Run it again!" one of the times, rather than relay someone in, so even the defense knew what was coming. That didn't help Joe's cause. Shortly thereafter, the clock ran out and the final score remained 30-0. What was next? Who won the other playoff? Who were we playing next week? Then we heard: Mooney had upset Moeller. At the same Rubber Bowl, we would play Mooney for the second time in six weeks, this time for the state championship.

Football is a mental game as much as a physical one and our mental state was very positive. But having already beaten Mooney, we may have been irrationally confident. When the scouting reports were distributed that week, there were only minor additions and no substantive changes to the same report we were given in week six of the season. "Mr. Ted Bell" still featured prominently. In retrospect, perhaps they should have been more specific about what the team was facing. Like the fact that as underdogs in the semi-final game against Moeller, Bell had run for 185 yards on 33 carries and that he was responsible for three touchdowns in the win. When added to his season total, he was over 2,000 yards. In just eleven games.

We had what might be called a sense of expectation that was felt, if not acknowledged. Practices were more serious than ever, and adding to their dreariness were ubiquitous snow flurries and steady winds. The game would be played on Friday, the day after

Thanksgiving, giving us an early practice that day with another admonishment not to overdo it – eating or otherwise. But in all other regards, the practice sessions were normal, perhaps too normal. We spent the week mostly practicing what had worked against Mooney just six weeks prior. Purely in hindsight: that may have been a mistake. Perhaps we should have reminded each other of our motivation the prior season in wanting to avenge our 1971 loss to Harding. Clearly, Mooney was not only a good team, but would also come into that game massively intent on avenging the defeat in the regular season. Their Coach, Don Bucci, admitted as much to the *Youngstown Vindicator* after the semi-final game. His declaration to his team was that the only way possible that they could get another shot at WWR was to beat Moeller, virtually citing that as the reason as much as any that they had cleaned Moeller's clock, and done so as the clear underdog. Mooney was on a mission.

But Mooney's coaches also realized that to win, they would have to change the way they played us. Bucci indicated this when interviewed by the *Vindicator*, following the championship game. He said plainly, "We made changes in blocking, figuring the Raiders' real (defensive) strength was in the two tackles and inside linebackers. So we went off tackle, to minimize the pursuit."[15] On the other side of the ball, Mooney's defense had already held WWR's offense scoreless in the first game, six weeks prior. It was Brian's touchdown from a fumble recovery that accounted for the only points scored by either team in the earlier game. They took what they felt were necessary precautions and made deliberate changes to how they would prepare for and play us on both sides of the ball. Mooney's offense wanted Ted Bell to get more freedom to run and Mooney's defense was already formidable, something Moeller undoubtedly now knew. This time they also had a vengeful chip on their shoulders. That and the "Chance favors the prepared mind" thing.

---

[15] Stolle, L.M. (1973, November 24). 'Bucci Lauds Great Mooney Defense in Garnering Title'. *Youngstown Vindicator*, pg. 11.

Pre-game warmups were eerily similar to the prior week. It started cooling off quickly again that day after the sun had set, but at least it had not turned bitter cold as it did the week before. Most everyone seemed focused and very little chatting went on between teammates. In the pre-game run-throughs, it was noticeably quieter. By the time we returned to the locker room, a sense of the moment permeated throughout. Guys made final adjustments to their uniforms. Officials checked players' pads and taping. This was a matter of routine to assure that no one was taping anything illegal above or below the tape or pads. All the while, everyone became more quiet and pensive. Slowly, everyone finished their preening and took a seat on one of the several long benches that encircled the room. Everyone was eerily quiet. We could hear the crowd's cheers, and the band playing as all of us were seated, staring at the floor, thinking about the importance of the game.

And then ... ***Riiiiiiiiiiip!!*** Instantly upon which, a dozen or more guys leapt from one of the benches screaming a few choice phrases, while Ed Manusakis sat alone in the middle of the bench with his chin in his hand, giggling his head off as his face turned redder and redder. In the dead silence of the locker room, Ed had just let loose the loudest sustained fart in the history of Ohio football. Mel Brooks would have wept. Instantly, everyone in the room including the coaches nearly collapsed with laughter. He could not have timed it more perfectly. In the seconds that followed as everyone regained their composure, Coach Novak just said, "All right, bring it in!" We did a quick cheer and ran out the door and onto the field for the last game of the year.

As we reached our sideline, a couple guys wondered out loud if Ed's faux pas was just the icebreaker the team needed to relieve the palpable tension. It nearly appeared so as in the first quarter, WWR recovered a fumble by one of Mooney's running backs whose name was not Ted Bell on their 21 yard line. Here Mooney, with backs to their goal line, foreshadowed the defensive prowess that they would demonstrate throughout the game. Unable to move the ball, WWR settled for a field goal attempt, but missed.

The fumble opportunity had literally gone for naught, and coming away unable to score the first points of the game was unsettling. The first quarter ended as a scoreless tie.

Early in the second quarter, each side had a couple short drives, resulting in punts. After Mooney's second punt, WWR returned the earlier favor by fumbling the ball away to Mooney, who recovered at WWR's 40 yard line. It took only three plays for Ted Bell to score the first points of the game, a Mooney touchdown. The score seemed to energize the Raiders, because the offense was able to drive the ball well following the kickoff resulting from Mooney's touchdown. WWR advanced well until reaching Mooney's 30 yard line, whereupon Mooney's defense, with their backs to the wall once again, stiffened. This time, Bill Williams' field goal was good, and the first half of the game ended with Mooney ahead, 7-3.

The halftime locker room was not fraught with panic. Even though we were behind, it was a close game. Adjustments, as always, had to be made. The defense had largely held its own, but the offense had been repeatedly stymied. Mr. Ted Bell alone had nearly as many rushing yards as our entire team did in the first half, but had only gotten across the goal line once. Once the third quarter started, something truly unique happened. Both Warren's and Youngstown's papers later reported that some fans had been stuck in traffic getting to the game. What they didn't report was that the reason there was so much traffic was that seemingly everyone from nearby Warren and Youngstown wanted to see this game. People kept flooding into the stadium well into the fourth quarter, until it would hold no more. Whether the Rubber Bowl decided to open its gates at halftime, or managed to sell hundreds of standing room tickets as fans walked up, the simple fact is that people were everywhere that they could possibly be inside that stadium. They just kept crowding in. The stated capacity of the Rubber Bowl was 35,000, more than twice the capacity of Warren's home field Mollenkopf Stadium. It simply is not possible that number, or the reported attendance of 30,000, was correct. People were rimming the walkways and standing in the aisles everywhere.

It is very likely that no team from Warren Western Reserve in its 24-year history ever played before more people than they did that day.

After the halftime activities, the third quarter was an exchange of punts on both sides. Stiff defense ruled the night for the most part. More punts were exchanged in the fourth quarter and, sensing we needed to move the ball, Coach Novak did what he probably didn't want to do, but felt necessary: he began to call more pass plays. Deep in our own territory, a Raider pass was intercepted and returned back to our 10 yard line. Our defense had little margin for error and saddled up in our short yard prevent formation. As Mooney attempted to run the ball with Ted Bell, he was stopped at the 1 yard line, but in doing so, he hurt his knee and had to be helped from the field. Another of their backs got the last yard, putting Mooney up 14-3 with very little time left in the game. WWR returned the kickoff well, advancing into Mooney territory, but desperate times called for further desperate measures, and four straight pass attempts fell incomplete. Time ran out on the defending champs. Mooney had won 14-3.

The defeat was bad enough, and we all just wanted to go back to the locker room, but state officials had other plans. As they set up the microphones for a presentation, I ran over to the Mooney bench where Ted Bell was laboring under near exhaustion and in obvious pain with an injured knee. Exhaustion, because he had accounted for 135 of Mooney's total 143 yards; all but 8 yards of their offense. Mooney's single pass attempt in the game was incomplete. Why would a team that had Ted Bell pass the ball? I approached him to congratulate him and shake his hand, but what struck me was that the only other human being anywhere near Bell was Neal Hall, our starting tailback, who had beaten me to him. No one - not a single person from Mooney - was anywhere near Bell. Not a teammate, not a trainer, not a coach. No one. That strikes me as unsettling even forty-nine years later.

Once the microphone was functioning, one by one, every player on our team was called up and presented with a runner-up plaque. We then had to take a knee and watch as every Mooney player was introduced, given a championship plaque, and have the state championship trophy presented to Mooney's Coach Bucci. The mood on WWR's side was somber but we obligingly watched the new champions introduced. Their defense had clearly risen to the occasion, allowing their offense to do more than enough to win. Bell received all the credit at the time, and while some of it is well deserved: the game was won by Mooney's defense. Their defense had held our offense scoreless in the first meeting six weeks earlier, and came all too close to doing it a second time on a cool Friday evening in November.

WWR had won 28 straight football games (regular and playoff) over three seasons. In those 28 games, WWR had outscored its opponents 647-111. But in the 29th game, the last game of 1973, the offense and the team, managed to score only a single field goal. Several of us, as part of the varsity team, had never lost a game up to that point. When festivities were finally over, we all just wanted to shower, change, and get back home. The mood was somber and there was very little talk among players as each went about their business. Everyone was trying to mentally process what had happened. When I was done, I walked to the back of the bus to be alone with my thoughts during the ride home, but two of the equipment managers were there, one of them laughing his head off, over and over again. Looking right at him, I said, "It's real funny, isn't it?" His lack of appreciation for the situation did not help matters, as he looked back and mumbled, "Huh?" I had had enough for one day. I got right up in his face and restated emphatically, "IT'S REAL FUNNY. ISN'T IT?" and then took the seat right in front of him. He remained quiet for the entire ride home. Truthfully, he was probably lucky I got there first and that I was just blunt with him about it. I know some of the other guys would definitely have not appreciated his laughing, but they would have almost certainly have handled their displeasure differently.

We would return to Warren as the AP poll state champions; the so-called mythical title. Generally, that's how we regarded it - mythical. No one talked about being the state champions. There was no massive celebration, no suspension of school for a congratulatory reception. Winning the mythical title was not what we wanted, nor what we set out to do. This of course, is the lesson that the world's foremost high-functioning miscreants had been telling us for years: "You can't always get what you want." And that is the essence of sports; perhaps the single most important life lesson that any sport teaches us. At the fall sports awards banquet, everyone got a chenille football indicating that we were the "UPI – AP Champs."

9

QUID PRO QUO

Each following spring, track and field season led to a few memorable moments and ultimately to a decision that was the equivalent of a fumble. One of the most vivid memories from track was of a baton exchange between Jim Browner and Neal Hall in the 440 relay. Everything was still in yards back then. 440 yards is essentially 400 meters, but the metric system hadn't quite found a comfortable place to call home in the Midwest at the time. The mile run was still called just that, not the 1500 meters you watch in the Olympics. Jim and Neal were both burners, two among several on the team. They were exceptionally fast for large young men, so they were the final two runners of the four man relay. In fact, we had so many really fast guys on our track teams that after a meet in Hubbard, their coach came to our bus just before we were leaving to congratulate us personally, saying that he had never seen anything like it, and adding that it was no wonder we had won the state championship in football. He was gracious, and we all thanked him in unison. Yet another act of sportsmanship that seems to have lost its way over the years.

The track spikes that sprinters used were just that: pointed, thin metal spikes of various lengths that screwed into the bottom of a lightweight running shoe, and could be changed easily with the proper tool depending upon the type and condition of the track. That day, the track had a conventional cinder/clay that called for the longest spikes available. On the exchange to Neal, who was the relay's anchor, Jim's track spikes inadvertently stepped on Neal's foot at the same time Neal was pushing off to build up speed while taking the baton exchange. Neal's final relay leg literally only took him a matter of seconds, but everyone was stunned to see a rooster tail of blood splatters all up and down his back as he crossed the tape. He had a huge gaping cut in his shoe, and into his foot, which sent him immediately to a hospital for stitches. But he had run his leg, and won the relay. And, since the track season wasn't over, Neal continued to run in meets with his stitches in a modified track shoe several times after that.

Jim often talked quite a bit that spring that it would be him and his brother Willard starting together in the backfield next season. He had been looking forward to that expectantly for a while. Jim played a lot at fullback, but shared time with Marty Murray, who would be graduating. Actually, both Jim and Willard had gotten considerable playing time at fullback and halfback respectively, but now the two brothers would soon start every game together. Jim had a genuine sense of pride about it, one that we'd like to think an older brother should have toward his younger brother. As it turned out, the fact that two brothers would start together in a backfield with championship aspirations would not to be the remarkable part of the pairing.

The other thing Jim was adamant about was that he wanted to play offense and defense and that was it. He said he didn't want to do what Ross had been asked to do, which was be on the field from the very start to the very finish. Few of us had thought about it before, but when you are as good as Ross - or Jim - chances are that you are assigned a responsibility in everything the team did on the field for the entire game. So Ross never came to the sideline for a break of any kind, and Jim didn't want that to happen to him. Guess how that worked out?

As a middle distance runner on the track team, 880 (half mile) and occasional mile run, I was more in my element than trying to compete with guys who bordered on being world-class sprinters. That resulted in being coached more closely by the assistant track coach ... who also happened to be the cross-country team coach in the fall. Persistent doesn't quite describe it, but he repeatedly asked me to run cross-country in the fall, to which I repeatedly told him I liked playing football. Once, to get him to stop, I said I might do it if I could do both. I was just being a smart aleck, but he just turned and walked away. We never really saw eye-to-eye and that was as much of my hesitance about it as anything. I understood where every one of the football coaches was coming from when they said something, or yelled, or whatever. Not so with this guy.

To build up stamina and endurance for distance and middle distance races, we ran through the neighborhoods, some of which had sidewalks and some didn't. We were told to run to Sabatini's along a specific route because he had clocked it in his car and knew how far it was (as I recall, two miles each way). Sabatini's was a popular Italian restaurant on the Westside, nearly all by itself across from a housing development called Palmyra Heights. On that particular day traffic was bad, so instead of running all the way down a long block and turning south on the short block, we turned on an earlier short block, then back east the exact distance on a parallel long block to rejoin his described route, which by the way, was the only road to get to the restaurant in the direction from where we were anyway. We did this solely to avoid the traffic, because part of his original route had no sidewalks. The city block was a perfect rectangle; it was exactly the same distance, just safer. My previously mentioned friend, Doug Dill, and I had recently both just barely missed being taken out on a road behind the school by a pickup truck with old style camper mirrors sticking far out from its sides. I leapt off the gravel shoulder that we were running on, out of the way, and straight into the ditch just a fraction of a second before the mirror would have hit me, and Doug who was just behind me staring at the ground as we were all prone to do as we ran, did the same thing purely as a reaction to my actions. So we had real reasons to avoid traffic.

The point of all of this is that, when we got back, the coach accused us of "cheating," being "lazy," and a couple other things that simply were not true. He had driven straight down the long block apparently just after we had turned at the earlier short block, whereupon he could not find us, and thus convinced himself that we were just hiding somewhere, because he did not bother to continue all the way to Sabatini's, or even just to look further down Nevada Street, where he most certainly would have seen our group running together. Every one of us told him what we had done and why we had done it, but then he absolutely refused to believe that the width-plus-length of the block was *exactly* the same distance as the length-plus-width of the block. I really got irate. First of all, I had just run every step of the four miles he wanted us to run. But I was so mad that a *teacher* couldn't understand simple geometry, that I probably swore at him a few times and I'm pretty sure I called him stupid, both of which I would never have done to any other coach. He seemed to be over it at the next practice. All the episode did was to get him to pester me a little less about cross-country. I think at some point he must have realized we were right ... it was exactly the same distance, and it was safer.

* * * * *

Real change was coming to the football team. One afternoon that spring, Coach Novak called an abrupt and unexpected meeting of everyone on the football team. There, he announced that he had accepted an assistant coaching position at Miami (Ohio) University; the same Miami University he had attended and where he had played football. He explained that he was leaving and why he was doing it, and then asked repeatedly if any of us had any questions. He did not want to let us down. He kept apologizing to us repeatedly, "If it was anywhere else..." and I'm sure with his coaching record, there had been other offers. Miami was the "cradle of coaches," it was the school and the program with which he was very familiar, and given his success as coach of WWR, it was the opportunity of a lifetime. We did not feel slighted or betrayed in any way. We were disappointed he was leaving, but wondered who would be taking the head coach's position. We did not have to wait long. Harry Beers had been at WWR from the beginning and would be the school's fourth head coach going into just its ninth football season.

In addition to Coach Novak, Coach Bud Myers left, along with coaches Morrison and Hinkson. Bud Myers leaving was a real problem for the team because he was defensive coordinator and a fantastic coach. Without his defensive adjustments in a few big games, we would not have had the trophies on display at the school that we did. But primarily, he simply was a great asset. His position players were well-prepared and as coordinator, his defensive squad knew exactly what was expected of them.

Summer came and Tuffy conditioning came with it. Two-a-days started without much fanfare. There was no new facility to show off or, technically speaking, any title to defend. But the goal still was to get into the playoffs and win the championship. A firm, if unspoken, resolve permeated the practices. We all still had the same championship hopes and confidence in each other. Still, something was different. It wasn't just that Coach Novak was gone, or that Coach Beers was any less capable. Everything seemed rote and routine. More troubling was that everything seemed to have been decided before any football equipment had ever been distributed. Obviously there were some no brainers. Jim and Willard were going to start in a backfield that would also feature greater use of the I-formation, and Bob Kascsak and Brian would start again on defense, just as Ed and Bill Huston would once again get their playing time. But we started doing basic formation set-ups and played non-tackle football toward the end of Tuffy - something we had not done the prior two years - and guys were already being directed into the first team offense to run the plays.

This immediately carried over to two-a-days. The lack of competitive opportunity bothered several players on the team. Before we ever did any actual special teams practice, I asked my position coach to be the holder on place kicks, e.g. field goals and extra points. I did so because I had often held and placed the ball for Bill Williams the prior year when he practiced kicking on his own. I had also done it, but only a few times for Bill Huston, who would obviously be taking over the kicking responsibilities. When I got a deceptively ambiguous non-answer, I immediately started asking myself why I was bothering. As always, it was late in the pre-season practices when we started organizing special team formations. Someone else was holding for kicks. School was about to begin and the season was about to start. Considerably more went into the decision making, but this prompted me to make it: I decided to run cross-country. I was among several who had been on the team for at least the prior couple years, but left before the start of the season, probably for the same or similar reasons. At least in my case, I did it to go do something else.

I came early the next morning and turned in my equipment to one of the student equipment managers who surprisingly had beaten nearly everyone there. Then I waited a brief time for Coach Beers to arrive. As he walked up to the Varsity House doors, I told him I had decided to run cross-country and that I had turned in my equipment. I did this specifically not just because it was the right thing to do, but also because Coach Novak had told the team that you don't just quit the team and not bother to tell anyone. Visibly irritated at the time he made the comment, I honestly don't think his concern was whether it was a player that he felt that he wanted or needed. It was the slinking out on teammates and ultimately yourself like a coward that offended him. Turnover (and apparently cowardice) had been prevalent both of the previous years and in all likelihood, even before that. I would not have slinked out of the building unnoticed in any case, for that was among many things which I felt Coach Novak had taught us about life, well before he specifically mentioned it. To his credit, Coach Beers appeared momentarily taken aback, then immediately said that that it must have been a hard decision on my part because he knew how much I liked football. I told him it was, genuinely wished him well, and he did the same.

For the football team, Collinwood was again first up, another home game and another shutout by the Raider defense. Austintown Fitch, Barberton, and Struthers followed, with Barberton being the first conference game of the year. The first four games were won decisively, with two shut-outs by a total score of 125-13. The Raiders were once again rolling, but the stars were aligning even more for a fabled showdown. Harding was next, and for the first time in the rivalry's history, both teams would enter the game undefeated.

There are less favorable and less appreciated aspects than first come to mind from the term "great rivalry", particularly if you are or have been a part of it. A great rivalry almost by definition cannot be entirely one-sided, or it's really not much of a rivalry. Someone has to lose. From the onset of the first quarter, that someone for only the second time ever, was WWR. Harding scored after the Raiders fumbled in their own territory, and then went to the air to score a second touchdown before the first quarter had ended. Reserve responded with its own pass attack, but couldn't convert after a touchdown, making the score at halftime 14-6.

Make no mistake, aside from frustrations at the tendency to lose to WWR, Harding had a good team that year. John Ziegler ran all over not only Reserve, but also several opponents in the All-American Conference, and Harding's quarterback Jim Richburg was as good as they had had in a while. A final Harding touchdown made the score 20-6. It should be noted however, that as good as their offense was, it was their defense that won the game. That season, WWR despite having championship caliber teams the prior two seasons, would set new team records for rushing yards, total offense, and most points scored. Against Harding in the fifth game of the season however, the team managed only 52 total yards of offense, and six points. Harding got the revenge they had sought, which spurred the team to a 9-1 season record. In beating WWR, Harding had book-ended the 29-game *regular season* win streak that lasted over four seasons, which had begun after Harding had won in week five of 1971.

Another illustration that things were different happened during this game. In order to slow the game down a bit, WWR had used up its timeouts in the second half. But at one point, as the team was on defense, a Raider player went down and was ultimately helped off the field. Coincidentally, the clock had stopped for this. After the game, I ran up to one of the equipment managers and asked how the player was. He gave a quick look of confusion, and then stated plainly, "Oh, he's fine, there's nothing wrong with him. We were out of time outs and they told him to fake an injury to stop the clock." I know who the player was, and I know he was only doing what he was told, and by the way, he put on a great act. I am pretty sure, but do not know for certain who told him to do it. I feel certain that such a ruse almost certainly would not have happened under Coach Novak.

How do you come back after such a disappointment? Three straight shut-outs. Monessen, PA was first up, followed by North East Ohio Conference opponents St. Vincent and Hoban, all of which failed to score a single point. The season was rounded out with Cuyahoga Falls and Lorain Southview, who both managed to put points over the Raider defense. But in the final five games, opponents had been outscored 140-21. WWR finished the season 9-1. More remarkable was that for the first time in Trumbull County high school football history ever, Reserve had two running backs rush for over 1,000 yards each. Even more noteworthy was that both of them were named Browner. Jim had over 1,200 yards rushing and averaged 6 yards each time he carried the ball. Willard made the 1,000 yard mark in the final game of the season. The two brothers virtually were the Raider offense.

While WWR finished 9-1, Harding had mostly cruised along until they faced down conference rival Canton McKinley. Harding was 8-0 going into the game. Keying on Ziegler, much as WWR had done with Ted Bell in 1973, Canton's defense held Harding's offense in check unlike anyone had done that season. Canton won 19-6. With a win the following week over Niles (also McKinley), that meant that both Harding and WWR had finished the season with a 9-1 record. *Jack Harbin ... are you listening, buddy?*

The OHSAA was to resolve the only burning question left in Warren after the football season ended. Harding finished in first place in Region 1, with the new method of using the total of only first and second level points. As illustrated earlier, third level points were no longer revealed, so we do not know what the final rankings would have been if those points were included in the rankings as they previously had been. What we do know for certain is that it can and it actually did make a difference in the rankings the first two years. Harding entered the playoffs and would travel to the Horseshoe in Columbus to play Cincinnati

Moeller in the semi-final game. Moeller entered the game undefeated and as the AP Poll Champions that year. A fierce game once again was saved by Harding's defense, which they won 20-10. In doing so, they earned a trip to the championship game and would face the also undefeated Upper Arlington at the Akron Rubber Bowl. Even today, Harding players will tell you that the hard game was against Moeller the week before. Harding's defense nearly shut out Upper Arlington on the way to a 41-8 victory. For the second time in the three years the OHSAA playoffs, the championship trophy would come back to Warren.

So:

In 1971, Harding won the last AP state championship before the playoffs began.

In 1972, WWR won the very first playoff state championship.

In 1973, WWR won the AP state championship.

In 1974, Harding won the third ever playoff state championship.

Four championship seasons in four years, by two teams whose fundamental shared goal perennially was to beat each other.

At the end of the 1974 season, WWR had still not ever lost a North East Ohio Conference game. Not one. This was both good and bad. It's nothing short of impressive that any team can go undefeated in their conference for five straight years. Barberton and Cuyahoga Falls were repeatedly tough opponents as was Akron St. Vincent, while up and down Hoban potentially represented a stumbling block or a close game. But with playoff spots dependent upon what amounted to strength of schedule, St. Vincent's saving grace was that it was in a conference with and otherwise tried to schedule games against Class AAA teams. As a private Catholic school, there wasn't a lot they could do about their overall enrollment, and so they were classified as a Class AA team. In turn, for the rest of the conference teams including WWR, this meant beating them resulted in fewer Harbin points - that's just the way it worked. Southview was another problem, because at least during this point in time, they weren't very good at all. Beating them, even if they were a conference rival, and no matter by how many points on the field, would not result in many Harbin points in the playoff rankings. A win gave you points, but a win against a winless opponent resulted in the absolute minimum of points you could gain, despite having beaten them.

10

PEERLESS

It's often said that football builds character. When your football team is full of characters, you're pretty much already there. Great football players were abundant at WWR. From this small city in northeast Ohio, players earned scholarships to noted schools such as Notre Dame, Ohio State, Cornell, and Michigan, as well as several other universities. As great as their on-field discipline and prowess was however, their individual uniqueness often set them apart. A problem with relating anecdotes of the wealth of personalities on these teams is that invariably some names will be left out. Therefore what follows should be regarded as one possible version of a top-ten list of peerless characters, starting with the one who – officially – was.

Ross Browner was recruited by dozens of major colleges in the country. I have no idea what he went through during this process, but I do know that the following spring the local newspaper had printed an article about Ross agreeing to go to the University of Nebraska. At the time, Nebraska was a national powerhouse, so it seemed that he had done quite well. I just happened to be in the locker room a couple of days later when he was talking to some friends telling them that he hadn't actually made up his mind yet. One of the guys there was a football teammate and asked him, "Why don't you just go to Nebraska?" Ross turned and said, "Cause they ain't got what I want!" Ross was a fantastic athlete and a true sportsman, but at that moment I realized he was also very serious about his future.

During track season that spring in which Ross ran hurdles, we were at a sectional meet, which is basically a track team's playoffs to see who moves on to compete for state championship in each individual track event. Our track coach was Nick Earl, who happened to also be my football position coach. Because schools from around the region came to the meet, there were many individual competitors for each event, which meant they would have to run multiple heats of each event. Most of the time they would take the top two or three from each heat and have a final heat among those heat winners, and then the top times move on to the next level of state competition. But the officials informed Coach Earl that everyone in every heat would be timed individually (unusual at that time), and only the best times – regardless of heat - would be eligible to move on. In other words, every participant would get only one chance. Because the hurdle heats were next up, he told me to go find Ross and tell him not to hold anything back and to make sure he goes all out. I may have given the coach an odd glance, but dutifully went to tell Ross, pretty much knowing what he would say to me. He was relaxing with a couple friends who were also waiting for their events, and I told him word-for-word what the coach had said, starting with "Coach Earl says" and ending with "go all out." Ross snapped back, "I always do!" at which I almost started laughing, but said, "Hey, I know that. I'm just telling you like he told me to do." He just grinned back at me.

Just five months later as a freshman, Ross started at defensive end for the University of Notre Dame. In his first game, he blocked a punt. Weeks after that, he was on the cover of *Sports Illustrated* (for the first time) among a group of several players gang-tackling USC's running back. Once again, it is important to understand that pre-ESPN, *Sports Illustrated* was it. *SI* was *the* authority of record for all things sports. Really, really famous athletes were on SI's cover, and now there was Ross. But the most amazing thing I ever saw him do athletically still largely goes unnoticed. In 1976 when Ross was a junior, Notre Dame played a good University of Pittsburgh team that featured running back Tony Dorsett, whose name was still being pronounced "DOR-set" at the time. He would ultimately win that year's Heisman Trophy. Upon that moment of notoriety, he informed everyone that thereafter his name would be pronounced "Dor-SET" because a friend had taken a French class and said that's the way they would pronounce it. Known for his quick moves and all out speed, highlight clips of Dorsett's college career still invariably show the break-out long run he had during that game against Notre Dame, with the voice-over marveling at Dorsett's ability to avoid tackles. What is almost never mentioned about that run is that the guy who caught and tackled him – *from behind* – was Ross Browner. Ross had never given up the chase, and very likely prevented a Pitt touchdown.

The following fall, *Sports Illustrated's* College Preview issue dated September 5, 1977 featured Ross alone on its cover with the words "Notre Dame's Peerless Ross Browner." Peerless is a pretty strong word, and in 1977 high praise did not come any higher in sports than to be featured solo on the cover of *Sports Illustrated*. He ended his college career being one of the most acclaimed linemen in college football history, and despite being a defensive lineman, finished fifth in the Heisman Trophy voting. In January of 1982, Ross played for the Cincinnati Bengals in Super Bowl XVI when, at the end of the game, the 49er offense was running out the clock to win their first championship. Playing defense as time expired, Ross greeted quarterback and former Notre Dame teammate Joe Montana who held the final snapped ball in his hands, telling him, "If I had to lose to anybody, I'm just happy to lose to you, buddy."[16] Ross was the consummate sportsman as well as one of the finest athletes ever to play the game.

The discussion of personalities might start with Ross, but the other name likely to be long remembered from the '72 team is Barry Simms. Barry radiated confidence and kept our varsity offense running smoothly week after week. Barry, center Denny Waltko, halfback John Hickman, Dave Sekerak, and a couple other players knew each other well and were seldom seen in or around school without one or more guys from that small group. Barry was an unquestioned team leader, one of our co-Captains, with a good, accurate arm. He was also seemingly unflappable. Once in a game, the exchange from Denny wasn't made for whatever

---

[16] Monanco, M. (2014). Waking the Echoes: Ross Browner, *The Observer*. Vol 48. Iss 42.

reason, but instead of dropping onto the ball to recover the loose ball (as we were repeatedly told to do), amidst all of the grunts and groans and linemen's feet moving mere inches from the ball, he calmly bent over, picked it up, took a short step back to plant and threw a touchdown pass to the spot where he knew John Hickman would be. Few things irritated Coach Novak on a regular basis, but one of them was Barry's inclination to seemingly take forever to warm up his arm before practice. "Come on Barry, that's enough! Get in here!" He wasn't being difficult; he would just take his time at it.

Another aspect of Barry's leadership that likely went unappreciated if not unnoticed was his play cadence. The ubiquitous cadence that we used, "Down", then "Set" to hike the ball, or start an activity or almost anything else, and which was heard every day by everybody. Coaches yelled it to start every drill, the scout teams used it (except in the rare instances where we were told what the other team did actually use), and of course our quarterbacks used it to start every play in practice and in games. For the most part everyone's was routine, rote and mechanical, but Barry had a distinctive take on it. His ever-so-slightly melodic *"Dowwn"* had a natural reverb to it that was confident and reassuring. It wasn't stretched out, it just reverberated. Metaphorically, if one were to attempt to spell the sound of his voice, you would cross over the two w's together, as if pronouncing them both at the same time. Through it, Barry's cadence provided direction and encouragement, no matter what the circumstances. In my experience, that's just how he was; he had no pretense. The picture that is most likely recalled from memory of the championship game is that of Barry near the end of the game giving Coach Novak a straight from the 70s 'right on' handshake. Even from the side you can see Coach Novak is grinning ear-to-ear, but Barry, looking at the photographer, has an unassuming 'of-course-we-won' look of satisfaction.

I first met Jim Browner in the seventh grade. Because everything was done alphabetically, and he being a "B" and I being a "C," we were in the same homeroom for the next six years.

Besides being a phenomenal athlete starring in football, basketball, and track, Jim was always one of the best dressed people in high school and a talented artist. Jim also later became versed in martial arts. Whatever his interest in it was, years later Hall of Fame running back Marcus Allen credited martial arts with helping his focus and agility, and said that perhaps more than anything, it helped prevent major injuries throughout his career. I suspect Jim benefitted similarly, but doubt that was the reason he studied it. Even in seventh grade, however, he was a big guy. My first direct experience was in a gym class, after which I twisted an ankle by foolishly hopping down to the stairway landing leading to the locker room. I didn't even get a chance to feel it out, because right behind me, Jim had seen what happened, grabbed my arm with his, and picked me up so that my feet barely touched the rest of the stairs, and then plopped me onto the first bench he saw at the bottom. As a senior, he starred in the backfield at fullback with his younger brother Willard at halfback, just like he told everyone they would. He followed Ross to Notre Dame and started at fullback as a freshman, switching to defense the following year. Just personal opinion, while I think he liked running the ball, I think he may have preferred hitting other people more than being other people's target as the ball carrier. He later joined his brother Ross on the Cincinnati Bengals.

Willard Browner was just a freshman in 1972, so could not play on the varsity team, but did as a sophomore in 1973. While Ross and Jim did track events in the spring, Willard played baseball, drawing interest from scouts for his athletic ability on the diamond as well. Before a football practice in 1974, several guys were just lightly stretching and moving around, with a few of them tossing a ball around. One of them tossed it to Willard, who was just doing light stretches standing with his feet parallel to each other directly on the goal line. Without planting or even moving his feet, he just flicked the football overhand to a guy who caught it on the 40 yard line. He made no more motion or effort than you would to toss a dog's toy across the room ... and the football went 40 yards.

In a late season game the prior year, Willard started getting leg cramps so they rubbed his calves down with something that was called "Atomic Balm." That was literally the brand name of it, right on the huge plastic jar that it came in. Basically, it created a heating sensation when it was rubbed on the skin. So, it was a general therapeutic for aches and pains and ... leg cramps. He went back into the game whereupon the team was immediately called for penalty. I actually recall that they called it unsportsmanlike conduct, a 15-yarder. The reason was because, even after rubbing it thoroughly onto your legs, it left a greasy sheen behind. Willard had to come out and the student trainers had to immediately clean every bit of residue from the balm off his legs and cover him up with new socks before he could go back into the game. Never saw that happen before or again.

Rick Kelly started at left defensive tackle and worked as hard as anyone on the team, because he loved playing football. He was never more than momentarily without his trademark smile. Given how hard he worked and how much he accomplished, you might never realize that Rick was also significantly hearing impaired. Although he wore hearing aids outside of football, I don't know how much they actually helped. You could have easily talked to Rick and not known, because he would look intensely at you, then answer you appropriately every time. You might just think he had only an ever-so-slight speech impediment, because I have never met anyone who was as good at reading lips. The other defensive linemen helped him out, probably none more so than Dave Zimomra. The starting linebacker and defensive captain would occasionally give Rick signals by hand and he and others also signaled to him that the whistle had blown and the play was over, if it wasn't obvious.

One time, a few linemen were hanging out in front of the school on a summer lunch break from two-a-days. It was either Mac Baker, Bill Pumphrey, or Larry Rihel who had one of those little British two-seaters (I think it was Bill), and was driving it around the flag platform in front of the school. Whether it was an

MG or a Triumph or whatever it was doesn't matter as much as the fact that it was a tiny little thing into which two adults could barely fit. The flag platform was fairly large, a little more than knee-high and floated above the concrete that the car was circling. When he stopped by where they were sitting, four or five of them, Larry Mallory among a couple others, each grabbed a corner of the car and lifted it up and onto the platform. Everyone started laughing and then, of course, most of them walked away. There was no way to drive that little car off the edge, and no way that just one guy could lift it back down himself. When they came back after a few minutes to set the car back down, they clearly had a little more difficulty with it the second time. When they had first surrounded the car, I didn't think there was any way they could lift it, and if I hadn't actually seen them do it, I probably would still think so. It was really a snippet of the entire team's mentality: they knew it was hard to do, but they were also determined to do it. They didn't stand there thinking or talking about it, they just did it.

A possible secret to Bill Huston's kicking ability was that, in addition to the square-toed kicking shoe, he wore six pairs of socks during a game - on both feet actually. He must have worn cleats at least a full size larger than his shoe size. There was no way he was going to stub his toe; he probably barely ever felt his foot make contact with the ball. On the track team, Bill ran hurdles and pole vaulted. We once attended a meet in Cuyahoga Falls that was a little different. Every field event had to have at least two participants to earn team points or something like that. Usually, it was just individual competitions in each event. So, I was a little surprised when Coach Earl walked up to me and said something like, 'You said you wanted to try pole vaulting - today's your chance. We need another pole vaulter, so just get Bill to show you what to do." Simple, huh?

Everyone knew Bill. He was very gregarious and would hang out with anyone who happened to be around. When conversations got boring, he would have us in stitches by responding over and over, "Is that right?" and varying the inflections each time. After a while, we would set him up to do it for a good shared laugh. Asking him to show me the finer points of vaulting wasn't awkward in any sense. I was not competition for him in the event and he understood the reason I was asking. The short amount of time was the issue. Seriously, it was literally: We better get over there and practice a couple times before more people need to use the vaulting pit to warm up. It ended up being: Okay, hold the pole this way, build as much speed as you can, and something I didn't quite get about planting the pole firmly into the vault box. Long story short; on about practice try number three, I didn't get the pole planted correctly, and halfway through the vault therefore realized that I didn't have enough forward momentum to reach the padded landing area; I was going to fall back onto the paved vault path. Fortunately, I had enough body control to try to swing my body out to the side as I fell back to try to avoid landing back on the pavement of the vault path, but Bill had other ideas. He was watching me from that side, and as I started to come back down, stepped in and made a perfect shoulder tackle. There I was, atop Bill's shoulder with the pole still in one hand. Of course seizing the moment, Bill had me firmly wrapped up and thinking it was hilarious, wouldn't let me off his shoulder. Then he started pointing to what I had done wrong, all the while carrying me on his shoulder. He eventually told that story over and over to anyone who would listen, and I probably really should thank him, because I was not going to land clear of the paved path.

The team's regular placekicker was Bill Williams. Bill played offensive tackle, but also had the distinction of having kicked Western Reserve's first ever field goal as a sophomore in 1971. The school had never once scored a field goal in its first five football seasons. As a result, Bill also wore a square-toed shoe during games and most practices. When he was free at practice and wanted to get reps, I often held the ball for him as he kicked field goals of various lengths. Given how few opportunities there were to practice kicking, it was surprising how good he was. In the first ever state championship game as a junior, Bill kicked two field goals, and fifty years later those two field goals still remain tied for the most field goals in an Ohio High School Championship game.

Joe Smith just lived in a different world from the rest of us. He would regularly talk about some girl, then a day later another girl, and so on. Any time we ever saw him with a girl, however, it was always the same one. He had a very easy manner about him, but for some reason, often tried to get someone to wrestle with him. That wasn't so unusual, what was unusual was that he tended to do this as he was on his way to the shower. He got no takers. Despite his slender build, Joe was a good defensive back known for sticking his nose into his tackles. When we adopted the 'Iron Eight Tight' defense for short yardage situations and Ted Bell, it was Joe who was moved up next to the line as strong safety and it was his play there more than anything, rather than as a deep safety, that singled him out. In 1973 at the fall awards banquet, Joe showed up in a medium green velour sport coat that was straight out of the 60s, a stitched and ruffled cowboy shirt, and blue jeans. Once again, we all just thought, yeah that's Joe. When the backs coach introduced Joe to receive his letter however, he said, "On the field, Joe played with reckless abandon ... and as you can see, he also lives that way." It got a big laugh, but Joe and several others didn't think it was funny. Anyone could see him visibly cringe, which is another reason why I remember precisely what was said, word-for-word. There was nothing about his appearance that was inappropriate, just the coach's need to make a rude and senseless comment on it, and it's the only time at any awards banquet or anywhere else that I ever saw a player mocked by a coach. This may or may not have been one of the reasons that coach lasted only one year on the staff. A couple years later, that former 'coach' tried to sell me insurance. Nope.

Willie Lewis was yet another guy that was fun to be around. Because we were both split ends, I was around him a lot. Willie wasn't distinctly larger, but he was solid head to toe, and that helped make him a good blocker. This was a good thing, because that's really primarily what the ends did. When we adopted the balanced line for a mercifully brief dalliance, he adapted very quickly to effectively becoming a tight end, because he was just a good blocker whether he was on the line or split out. Everything Willie did though, he grunted; in game or in practice, every time he made any kind of movement or action. So when a coach said "Set" to start a play Willie grunted "UH!" from his first step. When he made his cut to run the prescribed pattern, he gave another "UH!" If the ball came to him, there was another "UH!" as he caught it, and probably another as he turned to run up field. If he was blocking, there was a series of "UH!s" with every breath, once he initiated the block. All of this happened in a matter of seconds, so whenever Willie was in the play you got, "Uh! ... UH! ... UH!" A real 'people person', I ran into Willie at the Wendy's a year or two after we had graduated. He was with a girl, so I didn't want to bother him, but he had other ideas. As soon as he saw me come in the door, he waved, then jumped up and insisted I come over to his table and we joked together like it had been just yesterday that we had seen each other. A good athlete, it was guys like him that helped keep the camaraderie in the locker room and on the field. He had a genuine team sense of 'we are all in this together' that everyone appreciated.

Brian DeCree seemed confident and indifferent in his manner most of the time, but once on the field, a switch went on and you got a real football player. His brother Van had been a standout at Reserve and, concurrent with Brain's days at WWR, also at Ohio State, so Brian probably felt expectations that most of us never experienced. But he measured up, making the playoff roster as a sophomore. Because he did, everyone thought pretty highly of him. Once, we were on a bus ride to either a scrimmage or a JV game. We were both in the back, sitting opposite each other with our feet propped onto everyone's duffel of gear, which had been thrown into the aisle in a big pile. I remember thinking at that moment, 'Someday I'll be able to tell people that I was this guy's teammate.' But it turned out that was not to be the thing I remember most about Brian. One time, knowing this was just his way of doing things, he decided to test me. I was just standing against the cafeteria wall at lunch waiting for the bell to go back to class when Brain walked by and realizing it was me said, "Hey Carey, gimme a nickel." I just looked him straight in the eye and said, "I ain't got a nickel." Without a word, he started to turn away, and then I said, "But a got a dime." Visibly exasperated, he turned and said, "Well, gimme a dime then!" Half laughing, I gave it to him and he went off without saying another word. I'm sure it was a test, because had I not offered the dime, he would have asked me for money the next time. When he found out that I wasn't intimidated and that I'd give him the money, I'd passed the test. Although he saw me many times in the cafeteria after that, he never asked for money again. He wasn't rousting me; he was just playing a little mental game.

There were so many others unique in their own way who deserve mentioning, but you never get to know every single person on the team. The black guys tended to hang out with black guys, and the white guys tended to hang out with the white guys, but none of that was a hard and fast rule, and in many if not most cases it was completely irrelevant; we were a team. Players at different positions worked together, but did different things, which limited contact at times. But that never stopped inside tackle Chris Mason and split end Rick Houston from jawboning with each other regularly at practice. With exceptions here and there, most everyone got along with everyone else. Common purpose, coaching leadership, and joy in playing the game made this possible. Among others, Larry Mallory would have been high on anyone's character list, but these chapters are already peppered with observations of his antics. Starting cornerback Rick Peterson tackled me so many times while running pass routes on the scout team offenses that I think I developed a phobia about his number: 18. So many players were good athletes as well as great people. Without some, we might not have won as much as we did: Greg Patterson, and Chuck Aldridge, and Steve Ellis, and Danny Anderson, and Sheldon and Robby Beaver, and a considerable number of others.

I could spoil the party a bit and discuss a few of the rare times when teammates were surly, or jealous, or maybe just in a bad mood. Sometimes for good reason and for days at a time! However, that is neither my intent nor was it the norm for these guys. I have studied, researched, and taught university courses on leadership, team building, and competitive success. Succeeding as a team requires everyone to put aside their differences and work together for the common goal. If and when a team fraught internally with utter discord manages to succeed at their highest levels, it is contradictory to logic and reason, and their success is never long-lived. Nothing like that remotely describes or defines these teams.

The road to WWR's first playoff championship was enhanced and enabled by a number of other people and groups. Bob Harrah was a big, good natured, red-headed lineman whose father was a pastor at a local church. Often, his father officiated over some of our activities, such as leading the pre-game prayer, or giving the opening invocation at team meetings. He thus became our unofficial chaplain.

The trainers and student equipment managers deserve credit as well. They all put in long hours during the summer and were just as late or later getting home than we were.

But perhaps the most visible contributors outside of the team and coaching staff were the members of the Raider marching band. Throughout the August heat, while the football team was doing its two-a-day football practices, the marching band was also practicing inside the school and on a small grassy patch behind the school, or in the parking lot. Primarily, they practiced getting the music correct inside the building. Ultimately though, in order to perform their formations and their routines with the majorettes' dances, everyone in the band and all the majorettes had to come outside to get their maneuvers and timing down. We would occasionally hear them practicing, and that actually gave a little boost to our drills.

One day I was eating lunch during the break between practices in the shade of the gymnasium building; literally just sitting in the grass with my back up against the wall eating a sandwich. The entire band had been doing maneuvers with all of their instruments, but started to break up and, presumably, go eat their own lunches. Dozens of people left including the band directors, but about a dozen students stayed and seemed to be hemming and hawing, and then coordinating something between each other. I assumed they were working out something to get it right, just as we would run a play over and over to get the blocking or the timing or something else correct. Several of them started to line up while others stayed just to watch as a moment of hilarity ensued.

In a mocking, stilted manner, the formation jogged ahead to the drum beat quickly as if they were over-practicing a simple drill. What came forth however, was clearly an intentional parody of Harding's band playing their fight song. In perfectly imperfect exaggerated motions they played the fight song as if the band could neither hold a tune, nor hit their marks. But it was unmistakably Harding's fight song, and it was gut-busting funny. They had clearly prepared this all on their own and done it simply for their own amusement, perhaps to blow off steam while making the best of the rigors they too were enduring. For whatever their reason, more people should have been there to see it. I know Greg Foster was one of the instigators, he was in my class and was clearly giving others some directions before it started, and I noticed junior Raleigh Hughes banging on the bass drum, but I was laughing so hard, I didn't notice who else was there. Maybe this was a gag that they did at the drop of a hat, or maybe it was a right-of-passage for the band, as Senior Hit was for the football team, but that was the only time I ever saw it done. As soon as they were done, they disbanded and left quickly. It's possible it was something they weren't supposed to be doing and were afraid they'd get caught.

The majorettes, backed by the marching band, had a new dance routine for each home game, but would reprise their routines at away games. I'm given to understand that the show that featured the theme from *Shaft* was an enormous hit. There were nine majorettes, all of them excellent dancers and magicians with a baton. You don't get nine people doing coordinated dance moves week after week without a lot of practice. In four years of high school, I only knew one of them, because she happened to be in one of my classes. The reason I remember her mostly is because she was constantly getting comments from other girls about her eyelashes. "No they're real," Leslie would say, "My eyelashes are just long."

The cheerleaders also worked a lot harder than just yelling at the crowd on game nights. They painted the paper banners each week that adorned, or during Harding week completely obscured, the windows in the common areas of the school. That, all by itself, was an incredible amount of work. One week they must have used up all the paper rolls they had by painting banners with every single person's name that was on the football team including the coaches, in addition to the usual Go-Fight-Win slogan banners. Cheerleaders were fixtures at the pep rallies the day before most games, and the occasional bonfires behind the school, as well as Warren's Veteran's Day parade with the band and majorettes. And that was just during football season. Once basketball started, they typically had multiple games during the week to cheer. I never knew any of them nor had any classes with them, but solely because of being on the football team, many of them knew who I was and would say hi when passing in the halls. Cheerleaders put a handmade and handwritten message on every player's locker in the Varsity House during Harding week. They never got the credit they deserved for all of the work they did week after week. For what it's worth, "Thanks girls!"

It goes without saying that there were also athletic directors, and ticket managers, and groundskeepers, and maintenance workers, and game officials, and the cooks who volunteered to provide our meals in the summer, along with booster club supporters and many others who contributed immensely - most of whom we never saw.

Certainly, no one was more important behind the scenes of the glitz of the game than the players' parents. But perhaps as much as anyone, the community should give a special thanks to Mr. James and Mrs. Julia Browner. Of their eight children, four of their six sons would play in the National Football League.

There's a word for that: Peerless.

11

DENOUEMENT

Denouement is a French term that means 'the unraveling'. This is more appropriate than 'Conclusion', because there will both be some raveling and unraveling, rather than a definitive finish. Herein, we'll explore related odds and ends, calculations and facts, history and postulation.

One day in the weeks that followed the 1972 championship, I happened to go to Burger Chef on the corner of Parkman Rd. and Summit St. Don't bother to look for it, along with the entire franchise it has been gone for years. In fact, today there's just an empty lot where it once stood. In the day however, the fast food restaurant was a West Side booster that often had Raider-themed glasses and other school support materials available. That day, in front of the long counter was a drop box with a sign asking for donations to help buy championship rings for the team. It is the only place I ever saw such a sign, and I had not once thought about such a thing until I saw the box. Before you get too 21st Century in your thinking, be aware that at the time a high school class ring cost about $40. So we are talking along those lines, probably less, not a bejeweled Super Bowl ring costing five or six figures each. Shortly afterward, there was an announcement that the members of the playoff team would receive rings. Most of the sophomores and several juniors would not get them. Of course, as a group, the latter of us were mildly disappointed. However, when we later discovered that a significant number of school officials got them: the principal, the assistant principals, of whom there were three or four, as well as several other officials, disappointment morphed into a feeling of duplicity. It is this aspect of the issue that raises eyebrows, not the simple fact that a third of the players didn't get them. One should bear in mind that, in all likelihood, every person who donated at Burger Chef or elsewhere unquestionably believed that every penny they were giving was for the team and coaches.

This issue is precisely the type of decision-making that ultimately resulted in sending WWR and its achievements to the dustbin of history. The questionable allocation of championship team rings to people who had little to do with it is the issue, very much in the sense that had we eked out a winless record of 0-10 instead of 12-0, their jobs and their workload would have been virtually identical, unlike every one of the players and coaches who obviously earned their keep on the practice field, every day.

At the fall sports banquet, in addition to their letter, the seniors, juniors, and three sophomores on the playoff roster only, received a unique chenille patch in the shape of Ohio denoting the championship. Near the close of the awards, one of the assistant coaches announced that everyone would get a formal plaque of the second team picture, which was in fact very nice. Upon hearing that announcement, John Tackett, who happened to be sitting next to me, in exasperation said probably a little too loudly, "Finally ... we get something!" He was echoing what many of us were likely thinking. We are in the picture on the plaque with our names clearly identifying us as part of the team, but to save a scant few dollars almost 30 of us were denied a ring or a patch or both, the latter of which if I had to guess cost less than a dollar or two at the time.

* * * * *

Jack Harbin had made the simplest and most reasonable of requests. He wanted only to have his name put on the rankings as a simple - and thoroughly deserved - acknowledgement of his contributions. While his ranking system has been used in Ohio for fifty years and copied by other states nearly as long, virtually no one knows his name; perhaps because it disappeared from the official rankings in 1985 after just thirteen years. This is a travesty that should have been redressed years ago. Jack Harbin's passing in 2002 clearly illustrated how underappreciated, if not outright

172

disrespected, that his contributions had been. While Harbin was mourned by family and friends, Dan Coughlin noted that, "I saw no one from the world of high school football at his funeral."[17]

Here's a simple fix: Name every state championship trophy in every class or division in Ohio high school football the Jack Harbin Trophy. Do it before some fool decides to name it after a politician, or even worse, naming rights are sold year-to-year.

The rivalry between Warren Western Reserve and Warren G. Harding lasted just 22 years, but propelled both of them to the highest levels of state competition. From 1892 through the 1967 season, Harding had an overall winning percentage of 56.48%. For the period during which the rivalry existed 1968-1989, Harding's overall winning percentage increased marginally to 57.27%. Over that same 22-year period, WWR's winning percentage was a staggering 74.66%. Following re-integration of the two schools in 1990 up to and including 2021, Harding's winning percentage stepped up to 59.03% for those 32 seasons. In the 22 meetings between the schools, WWR won 14 times to Harding's 8, nearly a two-to-one advantage. In its 24-year history, WWR had just one and only one losing season. In the same 24-year period, Harding had 5 losing seasons, and in the 74 years prior to WWR's existence, Harding had 21 losing seasons.

Between 1972 and 1973 in his two seasons as WWR's Head Coach, Joe Novak had a 23-1 overall record, which included four playoff games. Perhaps more remarkable is that 23-1 describes precisely the sequence of that record. Novak's 23 wins are also the most consecutive wins under one head coach for any two-year period in the 130-year history of Warren high school football. The stellar 95.8% also remains the best winning percentage for any head coach in Warren's collective football history, both in terms of coaching tenure and *any* two year period. If one were to include the final five games of 1971 when he was an assistant under Jim

---

[17] Coughlin, D. (2010). *Crazy, With the Papers to Prove It*. Cleveland: Gray & Company, p.58.

Hilles, Joe Novak contributed to an unprecedented and thus far unequalled 28 consecutive game win streak (including playoffs). Between 1971 and 1974, under Hilles, Novak, then Beers, Warren Western Reserve won 29 consecutive regular season games. As if ordained on high, those 29 regular season wins were bookended by rivalry losses to Harding.

Let's examine some postulates of the "what if" type. As economists like to say, 'all other things being equal,' without the rivalry, it could reasonably be supposed that Harding's first undefeated season in 1971 would not have happened. Without the rivalry, Harding would have had no hated opponent literally in their backyard, driving them to avenge three consecutive losses. Even if they had somehow managed to finish undefeated, without that additional motivation, Harding might very well have been regarded as just another also-ran in the All-American Conference by the AP Poll writers – particularly given their extended history of mediocrity. We know that if the playoff system had actually started, rather than just been tested in the 1971 season, Harding would not even have been in the playoffs. They were topped in the test season of Harbin's rating system in Region 1 by Parma.

In 1974, despite winning the playoff championship, Harding did not win the AP Poll. But then, it took five years for the playoff champion to match the team chosen at the end of the regular season by the AP writers, so make of that what you will. In 1974, both Harding and WWR finished 9-1. Since Reserve's loss was to Harding, and if the two teams had not played, Reserve might have finished 10-0. Since WWR was second in Region 1 in 1974, they *might* have topped Harding by beating another team. However, it really comes back to the fierce competitive rivalry between the two schools providing the motivation to beat each other and then continue winning from there. Without the rivalry, it is simply very likely that neither team would have finished in the rankings as high as they did.

Without the rivalry it is highly speculative to envision exactly what might have transpired. But with virtual certainty, if WWR hadn't won the playoff championship in 1972, they would not have been voted the AP Poll champions in 1973. That simply would not have happened without the attention that the rivalry itself garnered, and the fashion in which WWR won both of its first playoff games. But under the Harbin system in 1972, and supposing they had not played Harding, it is possible they might still have topped Region 1. Likely opponents for their schedule might have been nearby schools such as Howland, Niles McKinley, or Hubbard; all three of which finished higher in the Harbin rankings that season than did Harding – a direct statistical inference that each of them was better that year than Harding. This implies that had they played any one of these three rather than Harding, WWR likely would have received more points than they historically did. So it is still possible, but less likely that WWR would have been in the first OHSAA playoffs. In 1973, however, all three of those teams finished below Harding in the Region 1 rankings. It's likely that the statistical volatility that would have necessitated the multiple schedule differences would have left WWR in the cold both seasons. The conclusion is that playing each other was the best possible scenario for both WWR and for Harding.

If there had simply been no playoff system, with the rivalry intact, Harding might still have won in the AP Poll in 1971. But even if it had happened, that would have been the end of it. Massillon was the AP champ in 1972. Having no playoffs to win that year, WWR would not have been named the AP champ the following year in 1973. It's much more likely either Upper Arlington or one of the prominent Cincinnati teams would have been named AP champ. In 1974, it was Upper Arlington who was the AP champ.

All of this supposition brings us to a thread debated often at the time. It was not at all uncommon for people around Warren to comment something to the effect, "Just imagine if there weren't two schools. We (a single Warren high school) would be beating everyone." There's a hint that this prideful boast might in some way be true, but upon reflection, evidence indicates that it is merely wishful thinking. In the first year of re-integration, 1990, the newly recombined Harding football team beat (ironically) Cincinnati Princeton for the playoff championship, once again (coincidentally) at the Akron Rubber Bowl. Even that year however, the AP Poll champ was not Harding, but Cleveland St. Ignatius. Thereafter however, Harding slipped right back into its volatile year-to-year pattern. But in 1990, the remnants and combination of the final years of the rivalry still fueled the motivation of the players on that team. Once the rivalry was gone, Harding's winning percentage for the 32 years from 1990-2021 effectively returned to just marginally above its pre-rivalry winning percentage at 59.03%. The difference was and always had been the rivalry. The construction of WWR and the rivalry it spawned between the two schools gave the city of Warren multiple champions that it likely –almost certainly - never would have had.

Post rivalry, Warren Western Reserve became irrelevant, then it became extinct, then it became an afterthought ... a footnote to Harding. In 1990, the schools were re-integrated back to Harding. Given continued falling enrollment, two public high schools in the city had become impractical and then unnecessary. Officials decided it was much better to send everyone back to the 64-year old building that was Harding High School, than the merely 24-year old Western Reserve. Surely, no one would subject the children of the city's gentry to attending a school where their poor cousins had languished. And remember, the decision was, as it was repeated before and after the announcement, "irrevocable."

The concession of renaming Harding's teams to the Raiders seemed just that: a concession. A token gesture meant to placate everyone whose history and ties would no longer matter. An interesting problem develops from doing this. Not the changing of the Raider's image, but the pronouncement of Harding being the Raiders meant that over time – an incredibly short amount of time - people will and thus have come to assume that all of Warren's Raiders were from Harding. People's memories are fickle; it doesn't take long to phase out something they didn't know or didn't care to remember in the first place.

In fact, there are sites on the *all-knowing* World Wide Web that identify Warren G. Harding as having won the 1972 playoff state championship, one of them with an asterisk that points to a minor footnote stating that it was when WWR was part of Harding. A disgusting thought to any West-sider, but foremost: It is simply not true. Another highly respected and well-known site identifies among Harding's alumni anyone named Browner: also not true. While researching what you are reading here, and as late as May 2022, there remains almost no useful information to find if you search for "Warren Western Reserve High School," other than perhaps class-specific reunion and classmate information. This brings oxymoronic meaning to the term 'virtual reality,' because there's *nothing* real about these examples, except that people accept them as true.

Apparently, not a single person, city or school official, or historical archivist has decided that the school and its memory deserve a Wikipedia listing, and one must realize even that is in light of the absolutely ridiculous amount of useless and petty nonsense that do have one. The city simply does not to this day understand what they had and endeavored to discard. The school and the rivalry it created *WERE* the reasons that there are any championships to celebrate or commemorate in Warren. This is what is happening right now: Very soon, no one will know the school even existed.

It seems antithetical, but the single greatest casualty of modern society is the truth. Not the truth as you'd like it to be: the truth. The official history of the NFL is that the Chicago Cardinals won the 1925 championship. While many sources exist to dispute that claim, if you would like a comprehensive look at why Pottsville's title may be valid and how they lost it, not on the field but by orders of the league president, I'd recommend a publication by the Professional Football Researchers Association in their Coffin Corner series entitled *The Discarded Championship*[18]. Not unlike the people of Pottsville Pennsylvania, the people, the

---

[18] Horrigan, J., Braunwart, B., & Carroll, B. (1981). The Discarded Championship, *The Coffin Corner*. 3(5).

alumni, and the city of Warren should embrace their unique legacy and their history, instead of trying to eradicate it.

All of this is occurred amid the backdrop of the ubiquitous high school experience. The hope for our individual and collective futures and the legacy each of us will leave or have left. The joy, and the pain, and the work, and the play of growing up and the pride in forging that future. Errant pickup trucks aside, the pain and risk of injury were lessened for me once I switched to cross-country. Nowadays, any lingering aches, pains, and injuries on my part are the result of misadventure by motorcycle, long after I had graduated from WWR. For others though, the pain persists, and each time a member of one of these teams passes, nostalgia nips at the heels of the memory of West Side Pride. We can and should be proud of what was accomplished on those fields throughout the week and on Friday and Saturday nights so long ago. Yet, for those of us who lived the Warren Western Reserve experience, our legacy is also being whitewashed, not just ignored. There is nothing where the school once stood but acres of grass and a few trees. I actually caught myself laughing in disbelief at the improbable. More than thirty years after it ceased to be, in a Google Maps view of the immense grassy lot that once housed the school grounds, you can still barely – *just barely* - make out the faint stripes of the gridiron pattern burned into the grass by years of lime where the football field and goalposts in the far southwest corner once reigned supreme. That faint outline, which is likely indiscernible to someone actually standing on it, is all that is left of the championship legacy of Warren Western Reserve High School. All that remains of Ohio's first state playoff champions. The school that gave the city a rivalry for the ages - and because of it, its champions - is no more, along with its memory.

Without Jack Harbin, practically no one would have known that Warren ever had a second high school, much less that such a school could possibly have been good enough to win the state's first playoff championship. It at least appears since WWR closed in 1990 that responsible entities have done nothing short of their best effort to make sure no one ever does know. At least that is how it appears. Whose fault is this? Is it the school and city officials who 'borrowed' the mascot name, tore down the school, and who obviously and deliberately failed to make any effort whatsoever to preserve a digital memory of the school, the rivalry, and the people who created its legacy? A legacy which energized a city for years as its industries and its economic base steadily declined. Or is it the fault of those of us who let them do it? It defies explanation, other than to say, perhaps we are all complicit. The people of Warren should be proud of the rivalry and the legacy of *both schools*, but those that would appear insistent upon minimalizing or whitewashing WWR altogether.

To whom it may concern: WWR's winning percentage in football was above 74% over its 24-year existence. Pick *any* 24-year period in Harding's history; it cannot be matched. A WWR memorial called the "Raider Walk" has been planned for at least the last decade. An earlier decision to include a statue of the Native American Raider has been reconsidered and revised to a scale three-dimensional depiction of Western Reserve High School itself. Even if and when it does exist, the walk will be placed on Harding's property. To properly honor the memory and historical relevance of WWR, this memorial should be - somewhere - on the west side. Since Harding's teams are now named the Raiders, this memorial will effectively subsume once again what was intended to honor the unique history of Warren Western Reserve into the legacy of its bitter rival Harding. It's true: We learn from history that we don't learn from history.

This is the hard lesson: Sometimes the future is cruel for no reason other than it can be. And sometimes the future is cruel for no reason other than we let it be so. *Ooh La La* ... you can almost hear Rod Stewart singing:

'I wish ... that ... I knew what I know now
When I was younger ...'

EXCURSUS

You may have noticed that I bookended the prose that I hope has both informed and entertained you, with allusions to the period-correct Faces song *Ooh La La*. Initially, this was done merely as an introduction to tug at collective memory by using a bit of popular culture from that time, 1973 to be exact, but it serves as an appropriate allegory. The image is that of an old man trying to tell an ostensible grandson some of the truths of life that he would like to pass on. But the grandson sees his tales as prattling about a time that seems ridiculous to him, even though the story and the advice that the grandad relates are true. But for the world and for the grandson, truth has become irrelevant over time.

Here's the allegory part: It is likely that anyone familiar with the song *Ooh La La* recognizes it as an early Rod Stewart song from when he was still the lead singer for the Faces. This is partly because the song has been part of his solo recordings and performances for decades. But the original Faces release of *Ooh La La* is sung by the song's co-writer: Ronnie Wood. Yes, Ronnie Wood: the Face who turned into a Stone (i.e. Rolling). Does anyone upon hearing the song *Ooh La La,* immediately think of Ronnie Wood? No. When the legend becomes fact, print the legend.

I don't blame you if you prefer any one of Rod's later versions of the song, but it's important to the story that you know who did it first. Just as important to know before it is relegated to the footnotes of forgotten memories – like the name Jack Harbin - is who won Ohio's first Class AAA state playoff championship.

It was Warren Western Reserve High School.

West Side Pride.

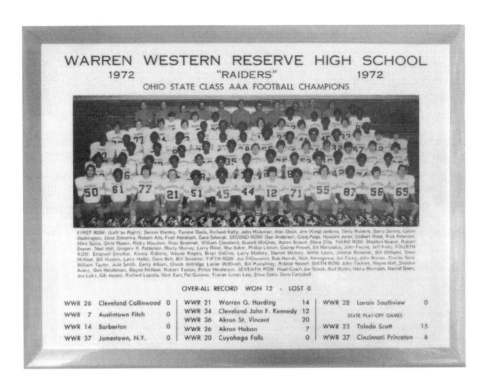

Photo of the plaque given to all members of the team. The team photo was taken early in the week before the first playoff game against Toledo Scott. A large blow-up of this photo was displayed by the school's snack bar and I remember thinking that, along with everyone else, my picture would be hanging in the school forever. It was not to be.

The complete 1972 team roster follows. This roster cross-references those pictured in the above photo with the names printed in the Fall Sports Banquet program (i.e. all those acknowledged formally as having been a football team member). Thus, the following list should be complete and correct.

1972 WARREN WESTERN RESERVE RAIDERS

OHIO CLASS AAA HIGH SCHOOL FOOTBALL CHAMPIONS
~ THE FIRST STATE PLAYOFF CHAMPIONS ~

Fred Abraham

Gerald Albani

Chuck Aldridge

Robert Alls

Nicholas Amorganos

Dan Anderson

Sheldon Avery

Malcom Baker

Robert Beaver

Sheldon Beaver

David Bell

Aaron Brown

Jim Browner

Ross Browner

John Bruner

Jim Carey

William Cleveland

Allen Davis

Tyrone Davis

Brian DeCree

Joseph DiGiovanni

Steve Ellis

John Fauvie

Jeff Foltz

Neal Hall

Wayne Hall

Larry Haller

Robert Harrah

Don Henderson

Ponce Henderson

John Hickman

Richard Houston

Bill Huston

Howard Jones

Robert Kascsak

Richard Kelly

Jim (King) Jenkins

William Lewis

Phil Linton

Darryl Mallory

Larry Mallory

Ed Manusakis

Chris Mason

Lanier McElrath

Burrell McGhee

Steve McNeal

Wayne McNeal

Matt Miller

Marty Murray

Robbie Newell

Joseph O'Grady

Craig Paige

Greg Patterson

Rick Peterson

George Powell

Bill Pumphrey

Delbert Reed

Charles Reid

Larry Rihel

William Ritter

Kenneth Roberts

Terry Roberts

Wayne Rogers

David Sekerek

Barry Simms

Joe Smith

Mike Spiva

Emanuel Strother

Bill Sweitzer

John Tackett

William Taylor

Robert Tipton

Dennis Waltko

Calvin Washington

Bill Williams

Dave Zimomra

183

1972 WARREN WESTERN RESERVE RAIDERS

COACHING STAFF

Joe Novak	Gib Jepson
Harry Beers	Dick Lascola
Dave Campbell	Joe Lukz
Nick Earl	Harry Morrison
Pat Guliano	Bud Myers

Pocket schedules for 1972. The sophomore
team played only Hoban and Harding.

1973 WARREN WESTERN RESERVE RAIDERS

The 1973 AP Champions.

Gerald Albani	Jeff Foltz	Marty Murray
Dave Alden	Neal Hall	Robbie Newell
Chuck Aldridge	Wayne Hall	Joe O'Grady
Nick Amorganos	Larry Haller	George Pappas
Daniel Anderson	Mike Hampton	Greg Patterson
Mac Baker	Bob Harrah	George Powell
Sheldon Beaver	Don Henderson	Bill Pumphrey
Robert Beaver	Ponce Henderson	Larry Rihel
Dave Bell	Bill Huston	Bill Ritter
Aaron Brown	Don Jones	Ken Roberts
Jim Browner	Robert Kascsak	Barry Schoch
Willard Browner	Willie Lewis	Joe Smith
Jim Carey	Phil Linton	John Tackett
Brian DeCree	Darrell Mallory	Bill Taylor
Joe DiGiovanni	Larry Mallory	Robert Tipton
Jeff Ditchey	Ed Manusakis	Bill Williams
Steve Ellis	Lanier McElrath	
John Fauvie	Steve McNeal	

In addition to Willard Browner, sophomores Rick Meigs and
Mark Jeffrey were added to the playoff roster in November.

SOURCES

Boissoneault, L. (June 19, 2019). The Cuyahoga River Caught Fire at Least a Dozen Times, But No One Cared Until 1969. *Smithsonian Magazine*. https://www.smithsonianmag.com/history/cuyahoga-river-caught-fire-least-dozen-times-no-one-cared-until-1969-180972444/

Coniglio, A. (2020, January 29). American Football League: The J5-V and J6-V Football. Remember the AFL. https://www.remembertheafl.com/J6-V.html

Coughlin, D. (2010). *Crazy, With the Papers to Prove It*. Cleveland: Gray & Company.

Edison, M. (2019). *Sympathy For The Drummer: Why Charlie Watts Matters*. Lanham MD: Backbeat Books.

Kelly, S. (2017). *Endurance*. NY: Mach 25/Penguin, Random House.

Hansen, J.R. (2005). *First Man: The Life of Neil Armstrong*. NY: Simon & Schuster.

Hatcher, H. (1949). *The Western Reserve*. NY: Bobbs-Merrill Company.

Horrigan, J., Braunwart, B., & Carroll, B. (1981). The Discarded Championship, *The Coffin Corner*. 3(5).

Jagger, M. and Richards, K. (1969). You Can't Always Get What You Want. Recorded by The Rolling Stones. On *Let It Bleed*. Decca; London.

Klemko, R. (2014, June 17). The AFL's Skinny Football. Sports Illustrated. https://www.si.com/nfl/2014/06/17/nfl-history-in-95-objects-skinny-afl-football-spalding-j5v

Lane, R. and Wood, R. (1973). Ooh La La Recorded by The Faces. On *Ooh La La*. Warner Bros.

Monanco, M. (2014). *Waking the Echoes: Ross Browner*, The Observer. 48(42).

Ohio High School Athletic Association. https://www.ohsaa.org.

Reed, T. (Writer), & Weaver, C. (Director). (2019, September 28). The Birth of the Ball (Season 1, Episode 12) [TV Series episode]. In C. Kuhn, P. Manning, & C. Weaver (Producers), *Peyton's Places*; ESPN Two; ESPN+.

Rosenstein, J. (Writer), (1997, July 15). In Whose Honor? (Season 10). In Rosenstein, J. (Producer), *POV*, New Day Productions.

Royal, D. & Sherrod, B. (1963). *Darryl Royal Talks Football*. Englewood Cliffs NJ: Prentice-Hall.

Rubin, J. (1973). *The History of the Ohio High School All-American Football Conference, 1963-1972*. Master of Arts Thesis, University of Akron.

Ruman, S. (2018, November 9). Harbin's Ratings Changed Ohio Football, *Youngstown Vindicator*. https://vindyarchives.com/news/2018/nov/09/harbins-ratings-changed-ohio-football/

Stolle, L.M. (1973, November 24). 'Bucci Lauds Great Mooney Defense in Garnering Title'. *Youngstown Vindicator*, 85(85), 11.

United State Census 1970. https://data.census.gov.

United State Census 2020. https://data.census.gov.

Warren Gridiron Club, https://www.wghfootball.com.

Wilson, B. & Gold, T. (1991). *Wouldn't It Be Nice*. NY: HarperCollins Publishers.

PHOTO APPENDIX

Warren Western Reserve High School

Billboard added to WWR's facade after 1972 season.

*Red arm bands distributed by the seniors on the team for Harding week 1972.
The score represents WWR's first lost to Harding in 1971.*

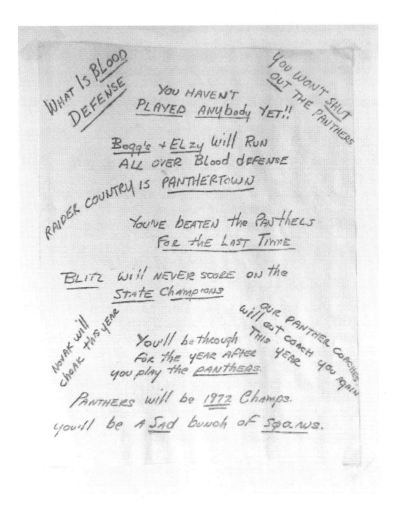

*One of the flyers dropped from a low-passing plane over the practice field
during Harding week 1972. They did the same thing the following year.*

One of the ribbons sold each week during the season.
For Harding Week, they were larger.
This measured 2-3/4 x 13 inches.

Excerpts from mimeographed 1973 Harding
scouting report follow (cover above).

OFFENSE

TE - #89 - Bill Shunkwiler - 185 - Jr.
 Both TE's are fair blockers. They attack low at the knees
 in a scramble technique. Both are very good pass receivers.

LG - #64 - Tom Zambelli - 186 - Jr.
 Likes to scramble legs, cross blocks well on backside.

C - #51 - Tom Day - 180 - Jr.
 Blocks well but does not sustain block, can be beaten on
 louie move.

RG - #60 - John Rubesich - 200 - Sr.
 Likes to scramble legs, will block down on nose a lot!
 Will pull a Belly Rt. (Z), on keeps and on pitches.

IST - #53 - Tony Angelo - 190 - Sr.
 Good blocker on blast tackles. Seals off inside well.
 Very good pass blocker.

OST - #70 - Nick Ahladis - 208 - Sr.
 Quick off the ball but does not sustain on pass blocking.
 Good cross field blocker.

SE - #42 - Jackie Hudson - 5'8" - 147 - Sr.
 Moved from WB to SE this week. Very fast and good at getting
 open. He catches the ball exceptionally well.

WB - #25 - Ron Culling - 190 - Sr.
 Very quick on routes. When blocking middle, throws low at
 the feet.

QB - #12 - Jim Richburg - 170 - Jr.
 Good ball handler. Runs belly pitch very well--can throw
 the ball deep and short. Puts the ball up for graps. We
 can intercept him. Likes to run the ball.

TB - #44 - John Ziegler - 188 - Jr.
 Has good outside speed, runs hard not a great blocker.Likes
 to get outside with the football.

FB - #32 - Kelton Dansler - 195 - Jr.
 Good blocker. Hard up the middle runner- fakes well.

FB - #36 - Jim Valentine - 198 - Jr.
 Hard nose, runs veer trap.Had great game against Stubenville.

DEFENSE

LE - #84 - Jon Hall - 180 - Jr.
Is fairly strong, good inside forearm. Not a punishing
tackler.

LT - #70 - Nick Ahladis - 210 - Sr.
Lines up lyd. off the ball. Executes an anchor move to
head of OST. Keeps head low. Better us run than pass.
His blast move is shallow inside the guards nose.

LLB - #40 - Ty Hicks - 165 - Jr.
Not extremely big but flows well to football.

MG - #67 - Terry McCoy - 170 - Jr.
Good quickness, has good move for football. Must sustain blocks.

RLB - #32 - Kel Densler - 195 - Jr.
Experienced blocker, extremely strong.

RLB - #62 - Bill Yarvorsky - 180 - Jr.
Strong boy, flows well to football, good on pass coverage.

RT - #77 - Bill Zeppsm 6'1" - 225 - Jr.
Very quick off the ball with a good blast move.

RE - #89 - Bill Shankwiler - 183 - Jr.
Plays a tough closing DE to our backside. Delivers good blows to
backs coming out of backfield.

Monster - #25 - Cullins - 190 - Sr.
Good hard nose monster, sets to strength of formation- will come flat
fairly well.

WC - #49 - Richard Hall - 154 - Jr.
Has good speed, will play away from monster. Good hitter, but can
be beaten on pass.

WS - #12 - Richburg - 170 - Jr.
Plays about 12 yds. deep. Has fair range. Gets nosey on run at times.

C - #42 - Jackie Hudson - 147 - Jr.
Has good speed, good hitter can be beaten.

The 22-Year Rivalry
Warren Western Reserve Raiders vs Warren G. Harding Panthers
~ Scores and Totals ~

	SEASON	WWR	WGH
1	1968	14	6
2	1969	30	0
3	1970	20	0
4	1971	8	15
5	1972	21	14
6	1973	14	6
7	1974	6	20
8	1975	20	30
9	1976	7	6
10	1977	6	7
11	1978	7	13
12	1979	16	7
13	1980	24	7
14	1981	7	24
15	1982	21	13
16	1983	12	7
17	1984	0	22
18	1985	34	10
19	1986	13	6
20	1987	20	14
21	1988	14	19
22	1989	42	6
	Total Wins	14	8
	Total Points	356	252

INDEX

ABOUT THE AUTHOR

Dr. James Carey was a member of Warren Western Reserve High School's 1972 and 1973 championship football teams. He has a Ph.D. in Business Administration and has taught organizational leadership and management strategy. He and his wife enjoy travel and have toured many parts of the U.S. by motorcycle.

My thanks to each and every one of the Warren Western Reserve Raider players and coaches who – during WWR's entire 24-year existence - created, sustained, and embodied West Side Pride. It was my privilege to be your teammate.

Jim Carey